JOSEF'S JOURNEY OF FAITH

Josef Herz

ISBN 979-8-88644-089-8 (Paperback)
ISBN 979-8-88644-090-4 (Digital)

Covenant Books
11661 Hwy 707
Murrells Inlet, SC 29576
www.covenantbooks.com

CONTENTS

ACKNOWLEDGMENTS

I would like to express my deepest gratitude to Robin Strom for her expertise in editing and valuable and constructive suggestions to the biography of: *Josef's Journey of Faith*. Robin's patience and hard work made it possible and are greatly appreciated in bringing this book to completion.

FOREWORD

This journey of faith tells the story of a boy, the youngest of eight brothers and two sisters, born during WWII, when surviving was not sure a sure thing. This young boy overcame against all odds and was afflicted with many common childhood illnesses. Allied bombings of German cities and factories intensified from 1943 to 1945 and caused hundreds of thousands civilian casualties, especially in the last two years of WWII. German women were frequently raped by the occupying Russian, American, British, and French soldiers after World War II. Soviet Leader Josef Stalin rewarded Russian soldiers for their hard-won victory, approving months of free reign to extract revenge on German women. Marshall Zhukov and Marshall Rokossovsky, after months of mayhem, issued orders to stop these atrocities. Zhukov's orders and measures were basic to all Western armies to their troops in their barracks and their hometown, as well as operations in a foreign country. The discipline and control exercised by British officers on their men in uniform kept those atrocities to a minimum. Finally, it must be recognized that not all Soviet soldiers took part in the free reign barbarism but had experienced and had been brutalized themselves and had lost their families by atrocities inflicted on them by the German Army and the murderous SS troops on Russian civilians, so horrible that other Allied armies could not even imagine.

After the collapse of the Nazi Regime in 1945 began the revenge killings of Germans on Germans, of neighbors suspected of collaborating with the SS, causing many of their neighbors to be sent to Dachau, the first concentration camp in Germany Proper, housing Germans suspected of being insurrectionists, clergy, and the mentally handicapped, and children born not according to Hitler's impression of the master race. "Undesirable" humans were removed by force from their families and communities, never to be seen again. Only months later, families received a death notice that their father, mother, son, or daughter had died a peaceful natural death, but there was no such thing as a "peaceful death" in German extermination camps. My parents managed to survive this mayhem and were able to raise their brood against all odds, relying steadfastly on God, Who promised that He will never leave us nor forsake us, Who will walk us through troubled waters, and even the valley of death. My purpose of authoring this book is to help people understand why trust in God in such horrible times was the only sustainable choice to endure, amid a catastrophic situation to overcome. Faith in God has strengthened and saved people for thousands of years against great odds. This book is about angel moments, too numerous to mention all in this book, which cannot be attributed to chance or coincidental luck alone, but orchestrated by none other than Yahweh, who has been at work through the boy's life even before his conception, and all through the nine months of pregnancy and birth. His mother was advised by the doctor that she would not survive another pregnancy, after already given birth to nine children. According to Psalm 139:15, God knew Josef even before he was born, and knit together in his mother's womb, and all through Josef's seventy-seven-year journey on this Earth. And all through the boy's Josef's life, from the moment of conception, God carried out His purpose for Josef despite the enemy's best efforts to destroy Josef. It is my firm believe that every human being will at one time or other experience trials and tribulations on their journey here on Earth.

We come into this world without our permission, into where and when, whether we will be born to rich parents or poor parents, respectable situations, or bad circumstances. When Josef came into this world, it was during the greatest calamity Germany has ever experienced in all her history, and the consequence of a murderous leadership, resting the power upon itself that belongs only to God, deciding who shall live and who shall die. During the twelve years Hitler ruled Germany from 1933–1945, 7 million Germans perished and hundreds of thousands died already prior to the outbreak of the war in concentration camps. If anyone objected to the human rights violations, they found themselves in the clutches of the SS and were at once send to Dachau or Buchenwald. But says Eliot, "But to apprehend the point of intersection of the timeless. With time, is an occupation for the saint—No occupation either, but something given and taken, in a lifetime's death in love, ardors and selflessness and self-surrender. That is our occupation now, is it not?" ("The Day After—The Catholic Thing").

And in a time of distress, may I suggest we remember the example of St. John Paul II and the difficult years he spent peacefully but firmly pushing back against the multiple evils he experienced in his days, first under the Nazi occupation of Poland and then forty-five years under Soviet subjugation of his homeland, when he reaped profound strength of character. That light shining in the darkness, though it may seem distant, should be for us like the star in Robert Frost's poem "Choose Something Like a Star": "The saint like the star asks a little of us here ["The Day After—The Catholic Thing"]. It asks of us a certain height. So when at times the mob is swayed. To carry praise or blame too far. We may choose something like a [saint] To stay our minds on and be staid."

After 1945, the Allied Occupational Authorities ruled over Germany, imposing their will on the German population. German generals and Nazi leaders convicted in the Nuremberg war trials were sent to prisons or hanged. The German population, in their desperation and fear of uncertainty, sought refuge in cathedrals and churches, praying to find strength amid the destruction that was clear everywhere and the agony of the bitter defeat clinging to God's promise that He would never leave us nor forsake us: "When you pass through the waters, I will be with you; and when you pass through the rivers, they will not sweep over you. When you walk through the fire, you will not be burned; the flames will not set you ablaze" (Isa. 43:2). This explains why after all the destruction and the loss of millions of lives, people turned to Christ Jesus for hope and restoration. The fact that I am writing my life story here today is proof that God and His angels were always with me. The picture on the next page reveals the desperation and destruction the civilian population endured at the collapse of Germany.

SECTION 1

From Time of Birth to Coming to America

1

JOSEF'S JOURNEY OF FAITH

The day of my arrival on this earth was August 18, 1943, the crucial turning point during WWII. It was proof that the German military might was not invincible, pointing to the first stage of failure of the "One-Thousand-Year Reich," so named because of the führer's conviction, foretold in the Book of Revelations, that Germany was to be the chosen Reich, to rule the earth for one thousand years, and Adolf Hitler chosen by God. Not surprisingly, he came to think this way because of over forty documented unsuccessful attempts on Hitler's life and his escaping every one of them. Hitler attributed his survivals to God's providence. Assassins ranged from a plain craftsman to high-ranking soldiers in the führer's own leading military command. By 1943, many German cities already suffered under the daily bombardments by British and American Bombers and were reduced to rubble. After the Battle of Stalingrad was lost, General Paulus was forced to surrender to the Russian Army, which fought the German Sixth Army from August 23, 1942, until February 2, 1943, for control of the city of Stalingrad in the southwestern Soviet Union. This was the bloodiest battles in the history of warfare, with an estimated 2 million total casualties, 1,100,000 Russian soldiers dead, 900,000 wounded, missing, or captured in the campaign to defend the city, and 40,000 civilians lost their lives. The German Sixth Army lost 650,000 soldiers who either died or were wounded. Ninety thousand survivors marched to

Siberian POW Camps, and only ten thousand, barely alive, returned to Germany. The year 1943 was the first stage of failure in Germany's dream to dominate the world for the next one thousand years.

German Soldiers marching to POWs Camps

The Home Front

Removed 2143 miles from that horrendous battle of Stalingrad lays my hometown of Wangen. The town was spared by Allied Bombers, but not from retreating SS units when they blew up the bridge over the Argen River, flowing close by our house, to prevent the French Army from crossing the river and advancing toward the city of Wangen. My father's house took a direct hit from the bridge explosion, and a boulder the size of a Volkswagen crashed through the roof and landed in the center of the living room. Because of this last fanatic stand by the SS, the French commander considered destroying our little village, but by the grace of God, a French woman living in our village convinced the French commander that the civilian population had nothing to do with the destruction of the bridge. The commander yielded and decided to spare all the houses, but only for their own comfort and benefit, after first expelling all the villagers from their homes, forcing them to live in makeshift shelters in the woods nearby. I am not sure how long this situation continued since I was only two years old and rely on my sister Josefine's account, who was twenty-nine years old that time.

The damage from the explosion was so powerful that a boulder the size of a small car left a hole in the ceiling of our living room, which my father and my older brothers tried to repair with limited makeshift materials available. What I remember most from those years was that food was always in short supply and eating potatoes and whatever else grew by the roadside and was edible. Our food was given to us by farmers from nearby farms. My older brothers, already teenagers and young adults at the time, became experts in obtaining foods from the French occupiers and even managed to recoup our eating utensils they appropriated from us. On a funny note, my older brothers filched from the French occupation force's beautiful pewter dinner plates and utensils. Since our house was heated by a little potbellied stove in the living room where we ate all our meals, if anything needed to be warmed up or dried, like socks or towels or work clothes, all was hung over the stove, and quite a few items ended up either burned or browned. Sometimes my mother would place a pewter dinner plate on the stove to keep the food warm, and within minutes, there was a hole on the bottom of the plate. So between the stove and the need for some desperately needed cash, most of our dishes soon disappeared, and from there on, everyone was handed only a fork to eat dinner with. This then became a catch-as-you-can situation, each for themselves depending on how much you could retrieve from the bowl. One day, the light dimmed, and as a result, a few had stab wounds on our hands.

2

PROCUREMENT OF FOOD

Children rummaging through the rubble of Berlin, hoping to find food.

When food became very scarce, my parents would send us out to beg for food from the surrounding farms. It was not referred to as "begging." Instead, it was called "Hamstern," bartering anything, even of little value, for something to eat as that was of utmost importance. Millions who once where rich or well off and had lost it all because of the war resorted to this way of staying alive, and there was at that time no stigma was attached to this routine. Farmers, by virtue of having to feed their livestock, fared better than folks living in cities and towns. When we were approaching a farm, we knocked on the door, and if the farmer's wife opened the door, we recited little rehearsed poems or sang children songs. This was our routine after school, when with a little knapsack on our backs, we walked to farms as far as fifteen kilometers from home. Kindhearted farmers took pity on us and handed us an apple or an egg or a potato. There were a few times when we would receive nothing, and it was then that we resorted to stealing anything that was edible. Fortunately, our region, being mostly agricultural, was dotted with many small farms, which were desperately in need of help, as many families lost their husbands and sons in the war, or they were still held captive in prisoner of war camps. Desperate for helping hands, they came to our family for help to bring in their harvest, and in return, they compensated us with something to eat.

City dwellers by the thousands, walking with knapsacks on their backs or riding bicycles for hundreds of kilometers, bartered jewelry or heirlooms for food. When I entered first grade in 1949, my school was 2.5 miles from our village, and it took us about thirty minutes or forty minutes because of clowning around on the way. Our breakfast consisted of a slice of bread with a little marmalade on it. In the wintertime, we marched to school in inadequate clothing for the high-altitude Alpine temperatures, entering the classrooms half-frozen and hungry. The French Army Columns, many soldiers having children of their own back home, were good-hearted and kind toward us children as they passed us with their tanks and jeeps and threw us candies and pieces of breads so sweet we believed it was cake.

Starting first grade, children carried a *schuler rantzen*. In my case, it was a leather bag that my seven older brothers already had used, holding a slate writing tablet held together by a wooden frame and a few chalk pencils. Paper notebooks and pens and pencils were at that time not available yet, and all assignments were written on slate tablets. Classes were held from 8:00 a.m. until 12:00 p.m. and from 2:00 p.m. until 5:00 p.m. Monday to Friday and Saturday from 8:00 a.m. until 12:00 p.m. Classrooms were filled with sixty students because of a severe shortage of buildings, and teachers were already in their seventies and eighties as younger teachers had either fallen in the war or were still held in prisoner of war camps in Russia, the US, Britain, and France and had not been released yet in 1949.

Malnutrition Caused Health Issues

US Army medical teams came to school, and after examining all children, they sent many to rehabilitation camps to restore their immune systems, compromised because of inadequate nutrition and the root cause of their ailments. By the age of seven, my health had deteriorated to the point at which boils covered most of my body and were extremely painful when touched. Fortunately, there happened to be a children's clinic nearby, and I was treated by a doctor who specialized in treating children with blood disorders caused by mal-nutrition. Many skin disorders were caused from a lack of hygiene, especially bathing only once a week in the same water the rest of the family already had bathed in, and afterward using the same towel used by the other siblings to dry off. Since our daily diets consisted mostly of noodles and potatoes, and few fruits and little protein, this may also have contributed to our skin issues. Mother sent my brother Eugen and me to live on my godfather's farm, and we could not have been any happier as there was always butter, cheese, meat, milk, and smoked meats for us to eat.

My godfather Benedict was a real shepherd, herding hundreds of sheep in the warmer months and joining his brother in the colder months working their parent's farm. Benedict was a real-life angel to us but also was grateful for all available help on the farm with the never-ending chores.

The region around Lake Constance, where I grew up, is famous for hops, cherries, peaches, apples, potatoes, and often at harvest time, farmers stopped by my parent's house to pick us up, especially when there was a change in the weather on the horizon, and time was of utmost importance to bring the harvest into the barns. Being so close to the mountains and the warm air flowing in from Italy, it made the weather unpredictable and caused it to change quickly. Thinking back to those years, and how by God's grace and mercy, and the good fortune of living in an agricultural area, food was grown and cattle were raised and a variety of wild berries were picked. Even though our yard was small, we also grew vegetables and berries and raised goats for milk and meat. That alone was not enough to feed twelve hungry mouths, but it kept us busy and fed. The millions of people who lived in the partly demolished cities scoured agricultural areas for food.

My parents did their utmost best to support all of us. Many summer vacations, I badgered my mother to let me ride my bike to the high Alpine meadows where farmers kept their young cattle for the summer and then back down to the lower elevation in the fall. The Alpine hut keeper (*hirtenwirt*) would watch out for the animals and was always happy to see me coming up for a couple of weeks, helping him with the chores and, in turn, giving me food. He let me sleep in the hayloft for free as this was my only chance to go away for vacation.

This type of accommodation was also popular with mountain hikers and climbers. When I was a little older and able to join a climbing party, I stayed in those huts for.50 cents a night. Because of a lack of electricity, the only entertainment was singing, playing cards, storytelling, and great camaraderie.

The Henry Morgenthau Directive

The Joint Chiefs of Staff Directive (JCS 1067) issued on May 10, 1945, which remained in force until July 1947, aimed at reducing overall German living standards to prevent Germany's reemergence as an aggressive power. This was catastrophic for the German population as it prohibited aid to the German agricultural sector and banned the production of oil, rubber, merchant ships, and aircrafts. This was implemented by the US following World War II to end Germany's ability to ever wage war again and, in the process, destroyed key manufacturing industries and food supplies. This directive inflicted untold suffering upon the German population, heaping malnutrition especially on German children and elderly who somehow miraculously managed to stay alive in their devastated cities and towns.

The Marshall Plan

General Lucius Clay, a senior officer of the United States Army, and George C. Marshall Jr., an American soldier and statesman who rose through the United States Army to become chief of staff, recommended that President Truman rescind and withdraw immediately the Morgenthau directive and implement the Marshall Plan. The initiative passed by US Congress in 1948 to provide foreign aid, primarily to alleviate the threat of starvation, and second, to reconstruct Western Europe, transferring $12 billion in economic aid to speed the recovery of Western Europe. It began on April 3, 1948, and ended in 1952, with the goal to rebuild war-torn Europe and prevent the spread of communism. The Morgenthau Plan was responsible for the widespread shortages of food for millions of families and their children. Beginning in 1949, French troops started to distribute stew and soups to schoolchildren, supplied by the Americans, and from there on, we not only had our little satchel filled with a slate writing tablet and chalk crayons, but we also carried an extra tin can school, begging the troops to give us a little extra for the night or to be shared with the rest of the family, and almost all soldiers gave us the extra.

As if I did not have enough issues to deal with, another problem created for me was by my seven older brothers who already had challenged many a teacher's patience. Many of them were recruited out of old-age homes to fill in the gap created by the absence of younger teachers. Upon entering a classroom, the teacher would ask all of us our names, and when they heard the name Herz, there was a sigh, "Oh no, not another one." But lo and behold, I was able to convince them that I was different from my older brothers. Entering fifth grade, my one year older brother Eugen joined my class because of him staying one year behind as learning was not his most favored activity. But now, the teacher had to contend with two of the Herzen's boys at the same time. I graduated from eighth grade "Grund Schule" elementary and middle school and was eligible to register in trade school as part of an apprenticeship program that offered me food and lodging. The only other choice would have been to become a day laborer. I finished my three-year apprenticeship program in a slaughterhouse and sausage manufacturing shop, teaching me how to butcher animals and produce sausages and marketing the products produced. One of the reasons I sought an apprenticeship at the butcher shop, or Metzgerei, as it is called in Germany, had to do with what I longed for the most, having meat to eat!

My mother was a magician when it came to cooking meals; she could turn anything that grew on the side of the road into something delicious, and if she could get her hand on any animal that at one time breathed, she could turn it into a delightful meal, with only one warning attached: never to ask or question its origin.

My father, a diligent man, rose every morning at 4:30 a.m., ate fried potatoes, and then rode his bicycle ten miles to work. He worked from 5:30 a.m. till 2:30 p.m. as a logger for a paper mill and then came home to eat a quick lunch and then left again to join a construction troupe, rebuilding houses or digging ditches until it got too dark. Just before the war started, my father built our house in 1938 to 1939 with my older brothers and his friends, as it was the custom when someone built their home. My father's brother was a Catholic priest who visited us often, not only to pray with all of us, but also to bring extra food and a little money to my mother. My father never attended mass or set foot in a church except for weddings and funerals, but because of his brother's insistence and my mother's devotion to the Lord Jesus, all of us children had to go to confession on Saturdays and Mass on Sundays. Religious education was taught in government mandated public Roman Catholic schools where the priests was anything but holy, inflicting severe corporal punishments on us children, often just for not remembering all the Catholic catechism. One priest, who was masochistic, enjoyed boys' bottoms as the object of his gleaming eyes and inflicted painful strokes with a rod. My brother Eugen happened to be also in my class, and to this day, refuses to put a foot into a church. From what we experienced, we concluded that these priests were not servants of a loving Father in heaven. Fortunately for me, another priest was so kind that when my first holy communion approached, he came to school and took me to a clothing and a shoe store and bought me a suit, shoes, and a shirt so I would blend in with the rest of the first communicants. I never forgot the kindness I experienced from that priest, but I also never forgot the cruelties experienced at the hands of priests who were priests for all the wrong reason. I have little knowledge of my father's religious experience when he was growing up or what his family was like. All I know from his side of the family is that his brother Franz became a priest, working after school in a sawmill and logging company. He was recognized by the owner for his devotion to Jesus and Mary, and the owner provided the means for my uncle Franz to go to seminary and become a priest. I have never met any of my father's other brothers or sisters. My father was born in 1897, one of eighteen siblings. At the age of seventeen, my father was drafted into the Kaiser's Army and served as a cavalry soldier the next four years, fighting on the French Battlefields in WWI.

My father was an unusually strong and tall man with hands the size of dinner plates, and we all knew that if we did not follow or obey his commands, he would use them. Fortunately, he hardly ever used them, and if he did, it was only if we refused to do as told. I remember vividly one incidence: My mother was very fond of red currant berries and had planted about fifty bushes, and during school vacation, we had to pick the berries. One time, I just did not want to spend all my vacation picking berries and left the patch. My reward for this disobedience was a spanking, severe enough for me never to ask for seconds. Every member of the family was expected to work and contribute to the needs of the family, whether it was picking berries or earning food credits from local farmers, as we were exclusively compensated with provision for the family table. To feed his family, my father leased a two-acre plot to plant potatoes, as this was our basic staple for nourishment. Every night, we would boil fifty pounds of potatoes on the stove and then had to peel them, so whoever rose the earliest could fry them before leaving for work. Eating potatoes twice a day every day was the norm. Fortunately, I really loved potatoes, especially as hash browns, or mashed, but also many other ways it could be prepared.

It is still a mystery to me to this day, and still I ask myself, how my father was able to raise ten children during the grimmest time in German history. Laboring in a paper mill, working second and third jobs, and still having enough energy left to build his own house. His mode of transportation consisted of an old bicycle, rebuilt from junkyard parts, which he rode ten miles to work each way. No wonder he did not have enough vigor left to go to Mass on Sundays? There were times when difficulties overwhelmed him, and he would the go to a *wirtschaft* (restaurant) to drown his sorrows in beer, but only on weekends, and never to my recollection did he miss a day's work. For us children, walking Saturdays to confession, and on Sunday to Mass 2.5 miles each way was an adventure, and doing what kids do when in a group. Faith in Jesus was a big part of my mom's life, and since my home state of Baden-Württemberg was 95 percent Roman Catholic, confession on Saturday and attending Mass on Sundays were the eleventh commandment and a requirement. My father, on the other hand, practiced his religion by being the breadwinner and enforcer of the work ethic he instilled in all of us. His word was like the high court; you would not dare to challenge him. My father taught us more by his work ethic, faithfully supporting his family, that we did not fully appreciate at the time, but we all profited from it all our lives.

3

THE SOUND OF MUSIC

Through all the hardships and struggles that my family had to go through in post WWII, music was a redeeming activity, and our house was filled with the sound of music. Our father played the tuba in a band and later organized his own band. He lightheartedly threatened us that if we were not playing an instrument, then we will not get any food. Only my two sisters and my brother Eugen were exempted from that mandate, and neither one ever played any instrument, but my older sister Josefine contributed by lending us her husband Paul, a gifted musician, who became our music director. Music supplied much of my parents' enjoyment, as well as us children, and it also augmented the family income. All boys were instructed by a musician friend of my father, who also helped to organize our own family band, soon playing well enough to be hired to play at town festivals in the immediate area.

A local folks dance group hired our band for all their festivals and offered financial aid in buying instruments and authentic Bavarian clothing. I thoroughly enjoyed playing in my family's band, even at the age of eleven, already playing gigs extending sometimes until 2:00 a.m. One not-so-enjoyable side effect to the merriment of making music, was the amount of alcohol consumed by many musicians, which led to violent disputes causing damage to trumpets, basses, and horns. And on one memorable altercation, a few teeth went missing from our leading trumpet player, who then played the clarinet. The overindulgence of alcohol was also responsible for many of our family arguments and disturbances. My father was, in all aspects, a loving father, and a diligent worker, but that changed when he drank too much alcohol, and he then became uncontrollable and, on a few occasions, very violent.

4

PARENTS TOUGHENED BY EXTRAORDINARILY CHALLENGING TIMES

M y parents were blessed with a strong nature and an even stronger will, and in retrospect, it was exactly what helped them to survive the circumstances with which they were dealt. My father, born in 1897, and my mother in 1903, both survived WWI and the ensuing devaluation of the German currency (Reichsmark). Millions of worthless paper money was required to buy a loaf of bread, caused because of the astronomical sums of money exacted under the reparation payments to the victors of WWI under the Treaty of Versailles (1919), which officially ended World War I between the Allied and Associated Powers and the German Empire.

The situation became extremely difficult as the unemployment rate reached 30 percent by 1932. The Great Depression that began in the USA in 1929 after the crash on Wall Street started in Germany already in 1919 after WWI, and reparations became so prohibitive and destructive that the victors agreed to suspend the reparation payments at the Lausanne Conference of 1932. The German people became increasingly desperate to support their families, but my parents managed to overcome anything the world could throw at them. My sister Josefine was born out of wedlock in 1926 as they could not afford to get married or live together. My mother continued to live on the farm where she worked as a housekeeper, but I am not sure where my father lived at that time. But finally, in 1928, they were able to lease a small farm and get married and live together. Times where hard, and for many men, alcohol was the soothing elixir to drown out their miserable situations, and like an American country song goes, "I am crying into my beer." Strength was measured by how many beers a man could drink before he would slide under the table, but there were few men who could drink my father under the table. If my father drank only beer, he would come home and peacefully fall asleep on the couch, but if he added hard liqueurs to the beer, he could get very violent. One incident I vividly remember was when my father came home one night inebriated, and my mother questioned him about his drunkenness. Things got quickly out of hand and ugly, and swinging an ax, my father proceeded to make firewood out of their new purchased bedroom set, which my mother purchased without his consent. Then in his intoxicated stupor, he gathered a few blankets and took up residence down by the bank of the river, which flowed close by our house. So we nicknamed him when he was out of earshot "cave dweller."

Recalling some of the moments could be material for a comedy show. In one incidence, my brother who worked in a brewery across the street from my father's favorite pub. My father was having a good time with a lady, sitting a little too close next to him, and my brother, wanting a beer before heading home, saw my father sitting so close to a lady. To him, it looked like something was going on, and he went straight home to tell my mother, who immediately mounted her bicycle and rode as fast as she could paddle to this pub. Without asking any questions, she proceeded to put an end to the liaison by beating the woman so badly that my mother was ordered by the court to pay the lady for her pain she suffered. Looking back, considering all that my father went through in his life, I cannot feel any animosity toward my father. Who am I to judge?

Fear of Poverty

Since my father experienced a harsh life, he could not tolerate any purchases my mother, or any of us, made without his approval, and we all knew the answer if we would have asked our father for permission. If my mother bought us shoes or clothes, mother instructed us to lie about where it all came from. Therefore, we constantly lied about the origins of whatever my mother bought for us, and we told our father it was given to us. And we really did receive many pieces of clothing from people who were aware of our circumstances. I would say that my father's fear and concern grew out of his fear of economic insecurity and instability of his earlier years and that was at the root of many disagreements in the Herz household. My father had a severe angst about not being able to keep his house and wanted to be informed and approve any expenditure for anything outside of an absolute necessity. As my siblings were getting older and bought a motorcycle or a car, my father suspected that my mother was subsidizing their purchases with his hard-earned money, and that, too, caused constant friction.

5

SUPPLEMENTING INCOME

My mother was blessed with an indomitable industrious spirit. She contracted with the agriculture laboratory to collect samples from the farmers' milk delivered to the dairies for further processing into cheese and butter. Our task was to fill little test tubes with their milk and list the farmer's name and number on the samples and record them. Some of the dairies could be anywhere from 6 to 10 miles away from home and at 2,500 feet elevation posed another challenge. To ride a bicycle especially in the winter with a wooden box filled with milk samples, which had to be delivered to the laboratory and then pick up another box for the following morning's collection. This every morning and evening five days a week. My brother Hans and Eugen and my sister Maria and myself were engaged in this endeavor to supply the necessary funds for mom to replace the bedroom set my father demolished and was also used to buy clothing and food. Later, it was brass instruments from that extra money as our band had increased to sixteen members. Another source of income was from farmers who frequently came to recruit us boys to bring in the harvest. I was called upon once to walk bulls to an auction where they were graded, traded, or rented out to impregnate cows. I was so scared of them, as some bulls were extremely mean, and every chance, they had come after me. Another time, a farmer asked me to drive a horse-pulled wagon to the dairy about three miles away from the farm. Everything was going well until a large tractor trailer came along and blew the horn. It spooked my horse, and he took off like a rocket, but luckily, I managed to jump off the carriage. Walking back to the farm, I discovered that the horse found its own way home without me.

6

EDUCATION AND TRAINING

Because of my father's hardships growing up in his family with seventeen brothers and sisters, where every child had to go to work full time after finishing grade school at the age of fourteen, my father also expected every member of his family to pay for room and board from the age of fourteen. Consequently, some of my older brothers and sisters were not able to enter apprentice programs and were then forced to work as day laborers to earn enough to pay to live at home. Higher education was out of the question because of the need for financial aid from what his children earned. I was determined not follow that route. Now, the only choice for me, I had to find a vocational training program that would provide me with food and housing, as well as professional training. After knocking on many doors and many rejections, I finally found a butcher and sausage business that offered me food and lodging above a cow barn, rooming with three other men, and it paid $1.25 a week. The room was heated by a little potbellied stove in the middle of the room, but no running water. All showers were taken with the cold-water hose in the sausage kitchen. Or you could jump in the street fountain nearby, which we availed ourselves of many times at night in the summer. Throughout my three years of apprenticeship, this was my home, and I was grateful to be trained, housed, and fed.

Two of my older brothers were able to start their vocational training because of the owners paying them a helper's salary for their physical strength and skills, which then was enough to pay for room and board at home. I, on the other hand, was a scrawny, skinny thirteen-year-old kid, and I am still wondering why my master had pity on me and would take me. The low wages of a *hilfsarbeiter* (helper) would not support a family, so I swore to myself that I would not fall into that category, so I worked toward of a possession of a journeymen's license qualification. My brother Walter worked many years as a laborer until he was finally able to enter a mason and bricklayer apprenticeship when he was already married and had children. His wife provided much of the income those three years it took to complete his training, and he then graduated with a journeymen's brick layers certification.

7

GROWING UP IN THE
CATHOLIC FAITH

My mother instilled in all of us that we are Catholic, and church was a crucial part for our lives. Another considerable influence in my years as an apprentice was Mr. Blaser, my master sausage maker, and his wife Martha, a woman who practiced her faith. Ms. Blaser took an interest in all workers in her husband's shop. She would even go as far as bribe every employee to go to confessions on Saturday and go to church on Sunday. Because of my meager salary of $1.25 a week, Ms. Blaser offered me an added $1.25 every time I would go to church on Sunday. The first Sunday as I left for church, she looked me over and kindly informed me that nobody from her household would wear work clothes to Mass. After I told her that work clothes were all I had, she took me Monday morning to a clothing store and bought with her money, a pair of shoes, pants, a shirt, and a jacket, so I would be properly dressed for church. Amazing how God works in mysterious ways! This happened to be the second time someone other than my mother bought me clothes for church. The first was the parish priest for my first communion and then Ms. Blaser. Her deep faith and her charitable deeds I never forgot. When she became aware that one of her poor customers had a newborn, she would send a gift, sometimes the christening dress and meat for the celebration. She practiced what she preached.

Battle of Conscience

About a year before I started working for Mr. Blaser, a former employee absconded meat and sausages and sold it to my mother. As faith would have it, one day, as I was walking home from confession, and freezing cold, a car stopped and offered me a ride home. It happened to be Mr. Blaser, and since my brother was good friend with one of his employees, he asked me if I ever saw that man bringing sausages to our house. Just having confessed my sins and knowing how much my family craved for some protein other than eat potatoes and noodles, I could not tell the truth about the sausages his employee brought to our house. As it turned out, Mr. Blaser became my master and benefactor one year later, and for the next three years, my conscience troubled me for all the years I worked and lived under his roof, and especially as he and his wife were my mentors.

Often, I would sit in church asking God to forgive me my trespasses and give me the strength to work extra hard to ease my conscience and that way pay restitution for the pilfered sausages. The work routine in Mr. Blaser's shop was extremely hard. We woke up at 4:30 a.m. and worked six days a week until seven, and many times past 8:00 p.m. A little reprieve came from the state mandate that all apprentices had to attend trade school one day a week from 8:00 a.m. to 5:00 p.m. My supervisor and some of the other journeymen made life extremely difficult for me. Even at night, since we all shared one room, they would come home drunk at 2:00 a.m., wake me and order me to find a kiosk (an all-night soda vendor) and get them a bottle of club soda or seltzer water to sooth their stomachs. Had I refused, some form of corporal punishment would be meted out for the slightest mistakes. This was a widespread among the teaching of crafts in Europe that the apprentices had to submit and was allowed by the trade guilds. For me, it became even more serious when my sister stopped dating my supervisor, and he committed violent acts toward me that left me no choice but report him to the trade administration who had oversight over the vocational apprentice programs when abuses turned too violent. Only because of their intervention was I able to complete my last year of vocational training.

Looking back, I am convinced, only my faith enabled me to bear those abuses during my vocational training and graduate. When the day of my contractual completion came, armed with faith, I left the company, and the following day boarded a train to the city of Duisburg five hundred miles away from my hometown, the furthest away my meager funds would allow me. Stashing my few belongings into a WWII cardboard suitcase, by faith, I trusted that God would be with me, and gave me the courage to seek employment with lodging. The ill treatment by coworkers was not the only reason for my hasty departure, it also had to do with my older brother Alois, who had many run-ins with the law, and his misdeeds and bad reputation made life extremely difficult for my me and my family.

Often, during my apprenticeship, my master would take me along to buy cattle for slaughter from the local farmers, and I was instructed that if asked my last name to give a bogus name. The reason being, if I would have told them my real name, I would have been chased off their property. Short four months of sixteen years, with only a few marks in my pocket, the German currency at the time (if converted from marks into dollars, a mark was only worth twenty cents), desperate as I was, nothing could prevent me from getting away from my hometown and start a new life. After an all-night train ride, I arrived in the city of Duisburg at 5:00 a.m., and then continued riding in an overhead electric bus to the town of Kamp-Lintfort where my brother Franz lived with his family, and my brother Eugen, who graduated also as a sausage maker one year earlier, found work and alerted me of another job opening in the same town. Visiting the central slaughterhouse, I happened to meet the owner of the sausage-making company, and after perusing my credentials in my journeymen's trade certification book that every job seeker was expected to present, I was hired right on the spot as a butcher-sausage maker.

8

NEW LIFE IN A STRANGE WORLD

My Southern German dialect presented a few issues for me since the Northern German dialect was quite different from my Southern Bavarian accent, and there were many occasions when I was oblivious to the instruction given me for the task at hand. Fortunately, my training had prepared me well, and I was able to perform any tasks necessary in the manufacture of sausage products, and in a brief time, communications also improved.

My new employment came with room and board, and for the first time in my life, I had my own room and was earning the large sum of 100 marks ($25) a week, for a fifty-hour work week. Finally, I was able to buy new clothing with the money I had saved up. I purchased a jacket, pants and a few shirts and socks, and a hat, trying to emulate those hats worn in the western movies and looking sharp. Now, my outside appearance was looking good, but as the Lord told the Pharisees, my inside was not so well. I was full of anger festering inside me, and going to church on Sundays I thought would help me to remove the bitterness built up during the three years of vocational training. But God, in His infinite mercy, sent me an angel in the person of a coworker who noticed how I was full of anger. He told me let go of it and not allow anger to poison my life and imploring me to let go of that anger, and God's prevenient grace made it possible for me let go of my bitterness. Reborn and free, it allowed me to concentrate on my future and seek greener pastures.

Living close to the largest coal mine in all of Germany was not exactly greener pastures, spewing out black smoke 24-7 from the hot coal. It was doused twenty-four hours a day and settling coal dust everywhere, even turning a white shirt grayish within two to three hours. Since I grew up in a fresh air Alpine environment, I decided to leave after one year and move to the city of Frankfurt, located near the Taunts Mountain Range. I was confident and again filled with faith, never doubting to find housing and immediate employment. Riding a streetcar to the central city slaughterhouse, heading for the cafeteria, the first man I approached was the owner of a large sausage-making company in need of an experienced sausage maker. A city of five hundred thousand people with an added one hundred thousand American troops stationed in and around Frankfurt meant six hundred thousand people in need of nourishing. Living and working near the entertainment center of town was for me a new experience, with four hundred nightclub famous for catering to GIs and German men in search of sexual encounters. With lights flashing in the red-light district all through the nights, I concluded that eventually it would become a snare to me.

Traveling On

My aspiration was to get to know more of the world. So in search to gain experience in my trade and knowledge of different sausage-making recipes, I decided to go to Paris and seek work and stay a year. Crossing the French border, the Gendarmes came, asking for my passport and suspected that I was a runaway criminal wanting to join the foreign legion to escape from the law. The French border guard took me to the guardhouse to see if my picture showed up on the German wanted poster list, but since they could not find an outstanding warrant from the Interpol out for me, they decided to believe me, that all I wanted was to come to France to gain work experience in my trade. To top it off, France was in the middle of a military coup to overthrow President Charles De Gaulle because of his granting independence to Algeria. Movement in and around Paris was severely restricted, preventing me from finding employment and not fluently speaking French made the situation worse and made me look more suspicious. Trying to negotiate my way around in the subway system and only speaking German, especially when asking for directions, as soon as the French noticed my German accent, they at once turned away from me. I expected some hostility since the war between France and Germany had ended only fifteen years earlier, and the people of France had suffered much under five years of German occupation. After two weeks, unable to find employment, I boarded a train again back to Frankfurt. One thing I learned from my France experience, crossing the border into France without being of the legal age of twenty-one, and without a work visa and no papers from my parents allowing me to leave Germany, was not such a bright idea. But I gained valuable experience for my next venture.

After my return to Germany, I immediately contacted my parents and asked whether they would be so kind to pay a visit to the town hall and file papers to have me declared legally twenty-one years of age, which my father was extremely happy to oblige. It released my parents of their parental responsibility for me, and within a couple of weeks, I received the paperwork proving that I was now legally twenty-one. Even though my France adventure could be seen as a failure, it taught me some important lessons; number one, get all the important papers in order. In the meantime, I also had met my future wife Roswitha, and together we paid a visit to the American Consulate to apply for a visa to make it possible for the two of us to emigrate to the US.

Meeting Roswitha and Plans to Immigrate to America

After my return from France, and desperately in need of work, I landed a job in a little village about thirty miles from Frankfurt, and there I met Roswitha. After dating one year, we were engaged in 1962, I embarked on a mission to convince Roswitha, who still had reservations about immigrating to the US. Lacking any relatives or a sponsor in the US, we searched for an organization that would sponsor immigrants with no relatives in the US. Someone directed us to the Protestant Relief Society sponsoring immigrants, and a meeting was arranged. The Protestant official asked us if we were Protestant, and we confessed to being Catholic, and he then kindly referred us to a Catholic Relief Organization with connections in New York, who then agreed to find a sponsor for us, for a fee of five hundred marks (about US $130). Returning to the American Consulate with the name of a sponsor, we applied for an entry visa and the all-important green card. In addition, the consulate required from all immigrants a US $4,000 deposit to forestall being a burden to American society. When the official inquired if we had the security money, I told them that I had most of it saved up, but in truth, we only had less than one thousand to our name at that time. The immigration process was still in the works, then in in May of 1963, the German Army ordered me to appear at the recruiting station for examination, meaning I would be inducted in a few months into the German Army. The day of recruitment came, and after passing the health examinations, I informed the officer that I already was in possession of a valid visa and green card and would soon be immigrating to the US. It was then another God moment when the presiding officer advised me to deregister at once at the German town hall since in Germany, everyone had to be registered at the town hall. He reasoned that the army could not send me the draft notice anymore to report to the army barracks. The officer recommended that I leave Germany at once, and following his advice, we did get married, and a month later, we boarded the SS *Maasdam* and crossed the Atlantic to America.

Shortly before our departure, Roswitha broke the good news to me that she was already pregnant in the third month, which added a little more urgency for us to immigrate to America. We could not afford even a two-room apartment in Germany at that time, and it came with the restriction, "no children allowed." I was at the time living with five other sausage makers in two small bedrooms above a sausage kitchen, and Roswitha was living with her parents, sharing a room with her twenty-five-year-old brother. This was one more motive to move to America where the possibility of securing an apartment according to our GI friends could be had for $75 and readily available. All that stress and anxiety caused Roswitha to suffer more epileptic seizures, and more than once, I had to carry her home. I have never been exposed to a person experiencing epileptic seizures, but one thing I was sure of that whatever was afflicting Roswitha, I would marry Roswitha, with money or no money, and immigrate to the US.

The funds to pay for the passage and paying for our wedding and still having enough money to start a new life in the new world was another hurdle to overcome. Money was tight for everyone. The pay for a week's labor as a sausage maker was not sufficient to support a family, much less to plan for a wedding and still have enough money to immigrate to another country. The only solution was to work extra hours. My coworker, who also was emigrating to America and just as desperate for extra money, connected with a farmer who had just opened a makeshift slaughterhouse in a converted barn and was in needed of help. Still working in our regular job from 5:00 a.m. until 4:00 p.m., we then rushed to work at the farm slaughterhouse from 6:00 p.m. until 12:00 midnight, catching some sleep for four hours, repeating the same routine before our planned departure. Weekends were a total disaster; I was so exhausted from that work schedule that I slept on Sundays until 4:00 p.m. in the afternoon. Church at that time was not on top of my Sunday things to do, but again, there was an angel coworker who hailed from Holland and who practiced his faith faithfully. Since we roomed together, he woke me up to go to Mass with him; otherwise I would have slept all day on Sundays. It was at this coworker's insistence that I could honestly tell the priest who connected me with our sponsor, yes, I did attend Mass some of the time.

Financial Struggle

Even with all those extra hours, I was desperately searching for more funds to finance the wedding and our immigration. In desperation, I withdrew all my social security contributions from the six years that I had already paid in by 1963, but it came with the caveat that I would forfeit my social security in retirement. As much as it was a gamble, I really had no other way left to pay for the passage.

Marrying in the Catholic Church

I was not eager to get married in the church, mostly because of the requirement of attending the mandatory marriage classes taught by a priest. I just could not comprehend how a priest, who never lived intimately with a woman, be able to tell us about marriage. But Roswitha insisted and refused to go ahead with the marriage plans unless we did get married in the church with a full Mass. I am forever grateful that she insisted to be married in church. The wedding celebration took place in the two-room apartment of Roswitha's parents, and we celebrated with enough food and wine, reminiscent of the wedding at Cana when the wine ran out and the Lord Jesus told them to fill all the jars with water and turned the water into wine. We celebrated until the early morning hours, and the wine did not run out. Neighbors and guests were kind enough to supply the food and gave us cash instead of wedding presents for the journey ahead.

Tearful Goodbyes

Four weeks after our wedding, the day came for our departure, and Roswitha's family and my brother escorted us to the bus station. Hardly any words were spoken. It was nerve-racking, as I was sure Roswitha's family was not thrilled about saying goodbye to their little girl being pregnant and not knowing where she would end up. But they walked us to the bus and wished us good luck. To be honest, I did not have a clue what was ahead. The moment the bus came was a heartbreaking moment, as Roswitha's mother and father were waving their daughter goodbye, hoping, but also recognizing, that they may not ever see her again. At that moment, doubts also came over me; did I do the right thing? Have I made the right decision, and what about the possibility of failure?

9

THE PASSAGE TO AMERICA

The bus brought us to the main train station in Frankfurt where we then boarded the overnight train to Rotterdam, Netherland, then calling a taxi to take us from the train station to the Rotterdam Harbor to board the SS *Maasdam*. Roswitha being pregnant in the third month, which is commonly known as the vomiting month, sure enough, during that bumpy ride from the train station to the harbor, she blessed the taxi driver with whatever was in her stomach. The cab driver was not too happy and demanded 50 marks to clean up the mess in his taxi; money we could hardly spare.

Boarding the ship and settling into the cabin assigned to us went well. Roswitha and I had never seen an ocean or an ocean liner before; you could say it was exciting until the ship was out on the open ocean. The date was August 20, 1963. Unbeknownst to us, it is also the time of the year for major North Atlantic storms. The passage through the English Channel was smooth all the way to Southampton, England, where the ship would pick up more passengers before heading out to the North Atlantic. But one day out on the ocean, the ship met such intense waves that the captain decided to seek safe harbor in Galway, Ireland, for two days. The rest of the passage over the Atlantic proved to be terrifying to say the least. During the entire passage, everyone had to be secured by ropes, even the dinner tables and chairs were secured by a chain to the floor. Most of the days, many passengers were too seasick to make it to the dining halls. Roswitha, after many attempts to join me for dinner, had to be escorted back to the cabin, unable to eat in the dining room. The ship stewards were on the lookout for Roswitha, holding the bathroom door open so she could quickly enter. God, in His infinite mercy, sent us another angel in the form of a cabin steward, himself a father of six children back home in Holland. He nursed Roswitha's seasickness with tea, crackers, and whatever else she needed to endure the trip. There were days when the ship was more vertical than horizontal, with the bow straight up and with the next wave pointing the stern down, repeating the process with every giant wave, which caused us to do headstands in our bunks, or in the next wave standing straight up in our bunks, according to the movement of the waves. I knew at that moment that if we made it to New York alive, it could only happen by the grace of our Lord, like when the disciples woke up the Lord when they were overwhelmed with fear on the Lake of Galilee. My prayer life improved dramatically. We tried to attended Mass whenever it was possible for the priest to navigate to the altar and celebrate mass. Occasionally it was impossible, and the priest had to retreat to his cabin after many failed attempts. Because of the violent Atlantic storms, the journey from Rotterdam to New York, which was scheduled to last eight days, but adding the layover in Ireland and the rough sea, lasted twelve days.

SECTION 2

New World in America

10

A NEW WORLD IN AMERICA

There are no words to express our appreciation when the Statue of Liberty appeared on the horizon, and the SS *Maasdam* finally entered New York Harbor and all passengers were clapping their hands. We had only $180 to our name to start a new life, without an inkling or knowing where we would find a place to sleep. We were painfully becoming aware that even a low-cost motel room was out of our reach and would deplete our meager funds in one week. Desperately, we started searching for the address of the convent on Eighteenth Street in Manhattan that the priest back in Frankfurt gave us as a last resort. Another angel moment, an immigrant from the St. Rafael's Society, consisting of previously immigrated Germans, had substituted for another volunteer who was supposed to pick us up from the dock. But because of his wife giving birth that afternoon, the first was unable to be there for us. So the substitute drove us to the convent, the few miles from the Pier 40 on Twenty-third Street where we disembarked, to the convent on Eighteenth Street.

When we rang the bell on the convent door, a nun came to the door and asked who we were and who sent us. Fortunately, the volunteer who drove us to the convent, already speaking fluent English, mentioned the name of the priest from back in Frankfurt. Recognizing the name of the priest, the nun invited us in and gave us an opportunity to explain our situation. In retrospect, there was a man named Josef with a pregnant wife seeking shelter. She may have recalled the nativity scene. The nun took us in and was kind enough to offer us a room for $8 a day. How, unless by the grace of God, was it possible to knock on a convent door in a foreign land and be invited in? Arriving in New York on that Saturday night, it happened to be Labor Day weekend. My coworker from Germany, who had encouraged me to go with him to America, had crossed the Atlantic four weeks earlier and was now sitting high on a pillar by the pier, waving frantically, and was accompanied by his wife, Roswitha, and their two-year-old daughter Angela. Their earlier arrival was necessitated because Herman's wife was already in the sixth month of her pregnancy and had to be aboard ship before the seventh month, the cut-off for pregnant women to be allowed to cross the ocean. My Roswitha was only in her third month of pregnancy, so we arranged to have our boarding passes exchanged, and we delayed our journey by four weeks. Herman and Roswitha were already living in an apartment in Brooklyn, and Herman found work as a butcher in a Manhattan restaurant.

Making Connections in New York

The priest back in Frankfurt had to be an angel sent by God. He linked us to the Catholic Aid Society in New York, a group of Germans immigrants dedicated to being angels by translating and finding an apartment and employment for the newcomers. One of their volunteers drove us to the Bronx and introduced us to a Croatian-German speaking apartment building superintendent in charge of renting out apartments in a forty-two-unit apartment building. There was one apartment available in two weeks but would have meant for us to stay at the convent for another two weeks. Again, God works in mysterious ways, as Roswitha passed out in their kitchen. The superintendent's wife was the angel to care for Roswitha, mothering and watching over Roswitha until she regained consciousness again. I am sure, the stress of the difficult passage and the uncertainty and fear of living in a strange land caused the passing out.

Again, a God Moment

The apartment manager's last name was "Mutter," *mother* in English. His mother, originally from the Black Forest in Germany, migrated in the late 1800 down the Danube River to Croatia and taught him German, which he spoke fluently. He and his wife insisted we stay with them until the apartment would be free. But when Roswitha woke up from her epilepsy-induced sleep, she was so scared that I would leave her with people she had never seen in her life before. We went back to the convent for the night, but they begged us to come back the next day and stay in their son's bedroom until the apartment would be ready for us to move into. Two weeks later, we moved into the empty apartment. Mr. Mutter and his wife and their daughter also lived with her husband in the same building, and angels sent from heaven. I will never be able to grasp the grace that our Lord had shown us those first days in America. Since we had no money to buy furniture, we slept on the floor until Mr. Mutter scavenged up a mattress, a table, chairs, pillows, and blankets that a previous renter had left behind, and within four weeks, we were living in a furnished apartment. Mr. Mutter also made me aware of a German language newspaper. Heeding his advice, I walked to the newspaper stand. Noticing an older man reading the German newspaper, I gathered up the courage and approached the man and began a conversation in German. He asked me if I was German, and what I was doing here in New York. And again, by God's grace and intervention, this man just happened to own a sausage manufacturing business within walking distance from the apartment we were waiting to move into. When I told him that I was a sausage maker from Germany looking for work, he was so elated that he hired me on the spot and asked me to come to work the following day. Thank God for the fifteen cents New York subway system fares, which made it possible for us to visit the Reffel family in Brooklyn. We often shared noodle and egg dinners together, or just potato pancakes with apple sauce. Those times we shared together were another gift from God as neither one of us had family in America, we became family and godparents to each other's children.

Roswitha was so frail that she experienced more epileptic seizures. Ms. Mutter was so concerned about Roswitha's passing out
that she assigned her son, a giant of a man, to go along with Roswitha
on her walks when I was at work. All these miracles convinced me
that this could not be happening just by chance or good luck, but
only by the grace of God. God in His infinite mercy provided for us
an apartment, a guardian family to watch out over us, and employment one block away—and all that right after our arrival. They say
in America, sometimes things are too good to be true, but this was
more than too good, and it was true. Sadly, one year after living in
that building, going downstairs to say "good morning," there was
dead silence. The apartment and their daughter's apartment were
completely empty. They must have disappeared overnight without a
trace, and to this day, we never had contact with them again. It was
a great loss for us since they were angels, there for us in our most
challenging time.

Mr. Mutter was very fond of wine, and on several occasions,
after being inebriated with much wine, he revealed to me that during
the German occupation of former Yugoslavia during WWII, he
cooperated with the SS and took part in the executions of Jewish
people in quite some gruesome detail. I could not be sure if he was
telling the truth or just bragging in his drunken stupor, but once
the whole Mutter family suddenly disappeared overnight, it became
clear to me, he might have been tipped off by a sympathizer that
the authorities were on to him. We stayed in that apartment at 145
Mapes Avenue two more years, as it was within walking distance to
go to work and do grocery shopping. We also came to know another
German family who lived in the same building, encouraging us to go
to Catholic mass with them and receive communion; looking back,
it had to be a family sent by God.

Employment

The German ham and sausage company was slowly going under
due to the owner's alcoholism and his affair with the bookkeeper.
Working hours were getting fewer, and I realized the need for other

employment. Pursuing a New York state driver's license was another obstacle to overcome and because of my inability to read English. I needed to pass the written test, which required sixteen correct answers out of twenty. Lo and behold, guessing the right answers, I passed the written test. To prepare for the driving test, I asked a coworker if he could teach me to double park into a parking space in two lessons, again I passed. Now, armed with a New York state driver's license, I went car shopping. With the $100 we had already saved, I went to used-car dealer and purchased a 1959 Ford Galaxy for $300. With a down payment of $100, the dealer allowed me to pay the rest in one year. The day I picked up the car, I felt like I just won a million dollars in the lottery. Roswitha, on the other hand, was sure that I had lost my mind. But she enjoyed the rides to the beach and parks, going anywhere just to get out of the hot apartment. Hardly anyone had any kind of air-conditioning units in the windows, just a small fan in the window. Folks would spend time together on the fire escapes to find some relief from the oppressive heat in the summer.

Now owning a car made it possible to search for work in various parts of the city, for a job that would give me more hours. The present job was dwindling down by that time to two days a week, and I was getting more desperate every day, as we tried managing to live on the bare minimum. Driving to a different Bronx location looking for a job, I came upon a ham factory, three miles from our apartment. Still unable to fill out a job application in English, I waited by a diner across the street from the ham factory, reasoning that one of the men walking across to the diner might be the foreman or the boss. Again, another one of those God's angel moments, a German-speaking worker came out, asking me who I was waiting for. I mentioned to him that I was a German sausage maker desperately in need of a job, and if he would be so kind, to ask his foreman if he could use a German-trained sausage maker. Without hesitation, he led me to a Mr. Piccolo, the man in charge of hiring, just going to the diner. With the assistance of the German man, I asked Mr. Piccolo if he could use a trained German ham maker, and he agreed to hire me under one condition, that I would be able to debone thirty hams every hour for eight hours, without leaving any meat on the bones.

Handing in my notice of one week at my place of work and then started to work for the new company, this was my chance to provide for my family. The supervisor was so impressed with my performance that he also offered me a chance to prove to him my ability in the injection technique of pickling of hams and added hours. All went well until the union steward came and told Mr. Piccolo that I could not continue working as there were other union men out of work with more seniority for upcoming openings. Fortunately for me, Mr. Piccolo already had made up his mind not let go of me. Working for that company for two more years, working from Monday till Friday, from 5:00 a.m. to 10:00 p.m. took a toll on me. I always thought that I worked hard in Germany, but it paled to what was expected here.

Many times, I cut myself very badly, but unable to afford medical treatment or miss even a day of work, I treated the injuries myself until I contracted blood poisoning from a deep cut in a finger. Also, the phosphate ingredient in the brine I was injecting caused my finger to swell, and a red streak developed up my arm. In desperation, I made a small incision, which allowed the infection to drain, and then I soaked the hand in Epsom salt, making the pain more tolerable, and not losing hours and my job. These injuries were quite common in this type of work until the union mandated that all workers had to wear steel gloves to protect their hands and their fingers, and a leather belt around the waist to safeguard the lower torso from more serious injuries. By that time Roswitha was getting more homesick and depressed and was not her usual upbeat self, pining for a visit from her mother, which would be a big relief for her. I visited the German Lufthansa airline office in downtown Manhattan and explained my situation to the lady behind the ticket counter. I inquired about the possibility of buying a round-trip ticket, paying half of it now, and when the time came for my mother-in-law to return to Germany, paying the other half. The counter person, after consulting with her supervisor, came back and handed me a one-way ticket from Frankfurt to New York, which made it possible for Roswitha's mom to come.

The Shadow of the Conflict in Vietnam

During Johnson's presidency, the US escalated its involvement in Vietnam, starting with the Gulf of Tonkin Resolution when Congress authorized President Johnson to use military force without declaring war, reinstituting the draft. In March 1965, the first US Marines landed at Danang. Men of my age were drafted and prepared for war, and soon thereafter, I received the notice to report to the draft office, and this, only four months after arriving in America. President Kennedy, in September of 1963, by executive order, halted the draft of married men by giving them deferred status, so single men would be drafted first and then married men, and last, married men with children. If I had been drafted and sent to Vietnam, that would have left Roswitha in a precarious situation, living alone in New York and no family for support. When our son was born in March 23, 1964, soon thereafter more young men received draft notices to join the men already fighting in Vietnam. By 1966, the war continued to escalate, and President Johnson called for more men to fight in Vietnam. Our daughter Sandra was born in September 1966, and I was downgraded again, thereby lessening my chances to be called to serve. As the war again escalated, increasing the need for fresh supply of troops, the Selective Service System of the United States resorted to a lottery system to determine who would be called. It was the first time a lottery system had been in use to select men for military service since 1942. For me, the draft lottery ended all likelihood of my going to Vietnam, and we could continue building a life for us in America. To be spared from being taken away from my family, especially as the death toll kept rising into the thousands, could only be possible by the hand of God. The directive by President Kennedy to delay the calling up of married men with children was another God moment, allowing me to continue working and being with my family. The cloud that was hanging over our head was another cause for the stress that contributed to Roswitha's anxiety and seizures.

The epileptic seizure episodes kept increasing, and again, another God moment, when our Jewish neighbors called Dr. Bernstein for us and arranged an appointment. The doctor's office was within walking distance from our apartment. After Dr. Bernstein examined Roswitha, he concluded that Roswitha suffered from epilepsy and devised a treatment plan to minimize the seizure episodes. So many God moments; the miraculous directive that blocked my involvement in a war that took the lives of fifty-five thousand young men and caused thousands to come back injured and disabled or suffering from PSTD (post-traumatic stress disorder) had a tremendous impact on my spiritual life.

Leaving New York City

As the employment situation continued to deteriorate in New York City and big ham-and-sausage producing companies relocated to Southern States where lower wages and the cost of doing business was less costly, two of the largest ham-and-sausage manufacturing companies relocated to Louisiana and Texas. Another big company declared bankruptcy, causing an added five hundred ham-and-sausage makers to be looking for work, which made my situation of finding work harder and more serious. Worries and anxiety began to rear its ugly head, and I was asking myself, "Now what?" Fortunately, at just that moment, a cousin of our German neighbor came from Connecticut to visit our newfound friends, and it just so happened that he was a sausage maker, and leaving his job. This created an opportunity for me to apply for the job he was leaving. The beef boning company he was leaving was in need for more experienced butchers for their growing business of deboning beef carcasses, which would require us to move to Connecticut. The German family we had befriended earlier also moved to Connecticut and invited us to come for a visit. Their cousin relayed to the owner of the company he was leaving, that a German sausage maker was looking for work in Connecticut. I received a call and an offer to start as soon as we could relocate to Connecticut, and again, God in His mysterious ways, provided.

While in Connecticut, our friends suggested we check out the apartment for rent six houses from where they lived. The owner of the three-family house agreed to rent us the apartment. Now, with the offer of employment and an apartment secured, we drove back to New York. I handed in my one week's notice to my employer, and the following Saturday, I loaded our few household goods unto a U-Haul. With Roswitha's mother still with us, we moved to Hartford, Connecticut. Then just a few miles before Hartford, a flat tire on the trailer endangered my meeting the new employer on time, as he wanted to speak to me before I was to start the following Monday. I, at once, unhitched the trailer, leaving my family by the side of the highway. I drove to meet the new employer for the face-to-face meeting. After the interview, I drove back to where I left my family and continued to the new apartment and moved in. The landlord welcomed us with open arms and invited us to Mass at St. Anne, a Roman Catholic church. Roswitha and my mother-in-law fell in love with the new apartment, so pleased that it came with a beautiful porch and a big backyard for our little boy to play. We did have more than sufficient reasons to go to Mass and thank God for all the help that came our way.

New Surroundings and New Working Conditions

On a positive note, moving from a forty-two-apartment block in the Bronx to a three-family apartment house on a tree-lined street, I no longer had to park on the street, where every morning parked cars had to be moved to allow the garbage collectors to do their jobs.

By contrast, I was now working in coolers and freezers kept at a constant thirty-one degrees, deboning beef forequarters and beef hind quarters at the rate of four quarters per hour, required to lift 150-lb. quarters off the rail to the workbench. Next, we would have to rehang the deboned quarter, still weighing 100 lbs. back up on the rail ten hours, six days a week. Mercifully, coworkers assisted each other when possible. The first couple of months doing that kind of work made my arms swell up and my feet freezing cold most of the day. I must have been the only person wearing long underwear and two shirts and sweaters all year around. I was grateful to have a job and able to support my family. This kind of work, difficult as it was, made it possible for us to save enough money for a down payment on a house and visit family back in Germany.

Boning beef is a hazardous job, because of working with extremely sharp knives. After many hours of cutting through chilled beef quarters, the fingers lose its gripping strength, but I still had to fulfill the quota. Many cuts and stab wounds resulted in blood poisonings, forcing me to seek medical attention. Working in freezing temperatures caused me to suffer from colds for most of the year. Seeking medical attention with limited health insurance, a coworker suggested I call on Dr. Hurwitz, an allergist speaking fluent German. Dr. Hurwitz treated me for a minimal fee of $5 a visit for many years. Much of our office time was spent in conversation about his beloved alma mater in Heidelberg, Germany, where he studied for his medical degree, which happened to be close to my hometown. Dr. Hurwitz also recommended that I seek a healthier working environment to prevent the onset of severe emphysema.

When the beef boning operation was about to be shut down, my German friend had purchased a German sausage manufacturing company and, now in need of a sausage maker, asked me to come to work for him. My dream ever since coming to America was to start my own sausage business someday, and the offer to work for one of the finest sausage makers was another gift from heaven. I needed the knowledge and experience to produce sausages with the ingredients and spices available and comply with USDA regulations. I recognized that all this could only be possible by the grace of God who introduced me to the German couple, Joseph and Maria in New York, and then to their cousin Bruno and his wife Christa, and a few months later, another German couple, Katharina and Franz, who moved into an apartment across the street from us. I am amazed at how our Lord works in our lives, and most of the times, and only when we investigate the rearview mirror of our lives, we come to realize that His hand was there all along. Being so young and having a family to support, and still learning to be a husband and father, has never been an easy task, but fortunately, Franz and Katharina guided us. Being people with a strong faith, and with the patience of angels, they were there for us and were role models for us to look up to and emulate.

We had many heated discussions about the Catholic Church, but Katharina, in her infinite patience, taught me the difference between following the culture versus following the teaching of the church. I must admit I was wrong more often than I was right, especially when Pope Paul VI, in his encyclical "Humanae Vitae" in 1968, strongly opposed the launch of the birth control pill.

Josef and Maria, who took us under their wings, became another family we could look up to. In faith and friendship, they advised us in financial matters, especially in the urgency to buy a home before it would become out of our reach. Inflation and the rise in the price of real estate would soon make it more difficult to own a home, and by their urging us on, we moved into our first home in January of 1968 in Tolland, Connecticut, which came with a beautiful lot. Our friends Franz and Katharina moved into the house next door already a year earlier, another miracle from God. Their children, being the same age as our children, played and went to school together. We babysat each other's children, skied together, and enjoyed unscheduled visits and were always welcomed. Years later, the May family moved to Colorado in 1975, leaving a huge gap in our daily lives. Fortunately, we still had our other acquired families in Ct. Herman and Roswitha, which we already knew in Germany; and they had moved up from Brooklyn, New York to South Windsor, Connecticut. Josef and Maria and Bruno and Christa were also living in Connecticut.

Soon, we made friends with Frank and Paula, a wonderful newly married couple, who moved in next door to us in Hartford. Paula, a writer for a local newspaper, was very instrumental in improving our English. We all became family and even called each other aunts and uncles and babysat each other's children and celebrated Thanksgiving, Christmas, and birthdays together. Many times, just getting together for a few beers helped us not to miss our family in Germany so much. But soon, we came to realize that we had developed stronger bonds here in the US than we still had in Germany. We joined the local German club, singing in the chorus, and participated in the yearly singing competition, winning many prizes, and attending their monthly affairs, dancing to German folk music and classic ballroom dancing, especially tangoes, Vienna waltzes, cha-chas, and polkas.

So even though we were far away from our German family, we felt right at home here with the life we made for ourselves in America. In many ways, the German club also functioned as a net-working center for members to find housing, work, and new friend-ships. On one occasion, going home after a night of dancing, we met a German couple who could not start their car and were looking for a ride home to Manchester, Connecticut. Since it was on our route home, we offered them a ride to their home and invited them the following Sunday to have dinner with us. Dieter and Marlise also had three children, and since they loved skiing as much as we did, we made many trips to the nearest ski areas together and became close friends. It was a sad moment when Dieter and Marlise announced that they decided to go back to Germany. Fortunately, we were able to visit them many times in Munich and are still in contact after forty-five years.

To our dismay, the family was not open to practice, or discus faith. Dieter even forbade his family from attending church. We always hoped, against all odds, that eventually they could see the need to bring faith into their lives and to their children, but to no avail. Even so, our friendship endured and was never in question. Visiting our family again in Germany, we bought a Volkswagen Camper and traveled five weeks through Switzerland, Austria, and Italy without breaking the bank on hotel costs and food, and we slept and prepared our meals in our camper. It was wonderful to travel with our children for five weeks, showing them the places where we grew up, and they got to see and know their grandparents.

New Opportunity

Upon our returning to the US, it became obvious that some-thing changed. The atmosphere working for my friend was not the same anymore, and I decided to seek other employment to secure enough income for the expenses that lay ahead, especially as our third child was on the way. When I approached my friend about an increase in salary and was abruptly turned down, the fog lifted from my eyes, and I could clearly see that something has changed in my absence. Pursuing other options for employment, and an increase in salary, at first nothing materialized, but then again, another God moment—my first employer in Connecticut called and offered me the position of manager for his wholesale and retail meat business, as his longtime partner broke up their partnership, and he desperately needed an experienced meat man. The remaining owner, who grew up in France and was drafted into the French army, had been captured by the Germans and then spent the next three years in Mauthausen concentration camp. My thoughts were, *How could this work? This man being Jewish and the horrible treatments he experienced while in the German concentration camp.* Trusting in God and my ability to do the work, I handed in my resignation to my friend and went to work for the Jewish man against the advice of all my friends. I would rate this career decision the best in my working life. The owner immediately took me under his wings and schooled me in how to run a wholesale meat company, dealing with customers, employees, and USDA inspection regulations, the government agency in charge of overseeing the meat industry.

I could never thank this man enough for all he taught me and the friendship he extended to me and my family, and the many times he invited us to the synagogue he attended and, in that way, opening our minds to the Jewish faith. The generous salary allowed me to save and invest for the future.

After managing the company for six years and growing it into a profitable operation, I felt secure enough to take my family to Germany and Austria on a skiing vacation. Our fifteen-year-old son, Thomas, stayed back to care for the pets under the watchful eye of our neighbors, Mr. Guertin and wife. Also, my friend Wolfgang who happened to drive by our house on his way to and from work, all were checking up on Thomas. Thomas spent the previous four months in Germany staying with aunts and uncles.

Arriving in Frankfurt, staying with Roswitha's parents for a few days, and then leaving Ursula and Sandra with their grandparents, we traveled by train to Austria to enjoy some skiing in the Arlberg

Mountain Region, near to where I grew up and went hiking in my youth. It was the off season, and hotels were empty, so that the inn-keepers invited us to eat with them in their family's kitchen. The following morning, heading up to the slopes and skiing a couple of runs on the lower parts of the mountain, Roswitha found the snow too challenging and decided to take an early lunch. I, on the other hand, decided to ski one more run from the top before going for lunch and skied down the mountain feeling good—too good, and a little bit too overconfident, when suddenly my skis hit a rock and snapped my right leg in multiple places. Now laying in the snow, and with no one within earshot in the higher elevation, I called out to God to send me someone to help, and nobody came for another hour. A peace that surpassed all my understanding came over me, nonetheless, that I can only attribute to God.

Because of my training as an EMT, serving years on the local volunteer ambulance team, I managed to move my body enough so that my upper body was elevated enough to prevent me going into shock. Then I used my skis and poles as braces to stabilize my leg, which eased the pain considerably until the ski patrol arrived to figure out the extent of my injuries and load me on a sled that hooked on to the nearest ski lift. They transported me down the mountain to the first aid station, and on to Feldkirch Orthopedic Hospital, about fifty miles away from the ski area. The accident occurred at eleven in the morning, and by the time I arrived at the hospital, it was 5:00 p.m., and two hours later, I was wheeled into the operating room for a three-hour operation. When I woke up the following morning, my leg was in a cast up to my waist, and I was unable to leave my bed. A teaching orthopedic surgeon professor was called at my request for an added fee of $3,500. Since I was not in possession of such a large amount. I phoned my employer back in the US and asked him if he would be so kind as to wire me $5,000, and behold, he wired the money to the local bank. The following morning, the bank manager personally delivered the check to my hospital bed for my signature. Another one of those "praise God" moments, trusting that His hands were underneath me, and that He would lift me up.

At first, my wife was not sure where the ambulance took me, and information was not very forthcoming in that part of Austria. But the innkeepers were angels, there for us by God, and they immediately invited Roswitha into their own home. The orthopedic hospital was seventy miles away from where my mother and my other siblings lived, and I called my mom. She was expecting me to be calling from Connecticut, USA, but once I informed my mom that I was in the orthopedic hospital in Feldkirch, Austria, she asked my brother to drive her to the hospital. Since I had not seen my mother in four years, I was astonished to see my mother frail and not the way I remembered my mother, being a stately woman, and now so frail. After being kept one week in the hospital, I was ready to be released, and so my brother came to transport Roswitha and me to my mother's house. Staying there for a few days, we then went on by train to Frankfurt. Trains are notorious for their narrow pathways and small cabins and tiny restrooms, presenting a big challenge, and a five-hour ordeal. The restroom proved to be the biggest challenge, being on full display with my leg in a cast extending out into the hallway. I was unable to close the door,.

Roswitha tried her best to block the view as much as possible, but with the train moving and shaking, it made her unsteady on her feet. It could be aptly called a train show. Finally arriving in Frankfurt, my brother Eugen drove us by car to my brother-in-law's house, where we stayed until the time came to go to Frankfurt Airport. The airline supplied a people transporter that supported my stretched-out leg and took all of us to the boarding area and on to the plane and our seats, and even provided enough room for my extended leg. After the eight-hour flight from Frankfurt to New York, just getting me off the plane and through customs was a traumatic experience. We went to retrieve our luggage and lugging it to the car rental office to rent a station wagon and fashioned a makeshift bed using the luggage and the skis for stabilization. Since it was late January and snowing heavily all the way to Connecticut, my courageous wife put her big girl pants on and drove to us safely home in poor road conditions. Then, faced with a big pile of snow blocking the driveway, Roswitha, rising again for the challenge, and with all of us fervently praying the "Hail

Mary," gunned the car and literally flew over the snowbank straight into the garage, and by God's grace, we landed without a scratch safely inside the house.

Then the next big challenge was, how would I make it from the garage up the stairs and to the bedroom? The excruciating pains I experienced all throughout the journey were due to the fact that the cast was wrapped around the wounds without protective material to prevent the cast from sticking to my incisions, and every movement caused a lot of pain in my leg. But with much screaming, we made it up the stairs and finally to my own bed. The following week was a repeat of the painful encounter, getting to the orthopedic surgeon's office for the replacing of the cast. As the doctor was cutting away the old cast, I let out a scream because he was cutting into my leg, not being aware that there was no protective padding under the cast. Then came the prognosis that it would take one year for me to use that leg again and require more surgery to remove all the wiring that held the comminuted fracture together. I became a firm believer in the adage, "If it does not kill you, it will make you stronger," and by God's grace, it did make me stronger and able to overcome whatever came my way. Still desperately in need of going back to work and still in a lot of pain, I managed to drive with my good left leg crossed over to reach the brake and the gas pedal, with the injured right leg resting on the bench seat common in sedans and drove this way every day to the office.

My employer Wilbert, the angel that he was, allowed me to manage and supervise the operation from the office as well as I could. In that way, I was able to work through the entire year, except when I had to go to the hospital or doctor visits. Arriving at my place of work, another angel came to my aid, a big and strong black man who worked for the company, who carried me from the car to the office, and then back to the car at the end of the day. But driving with the left foot was not an ideal or a safe way to drive a car. There was one time when the car in front of me came to a sudden stop, and my good left leg was in an awkward position relative to the brake pedal so that in my fear and angst, I ripped the shoe from my foot. The shoe was hung up underneath the brake pedal, and again by God's grace, I came to a stop at the last second without hitting the car in front on me. I was so shaken up that I had to pull over to the side of the road until I was able to stop shaking. God was with me every step of the way. This way of driving went on until November, when the doctor finally operated and removed all the wiring. And finally, without the cast, I was able to drive the normal way again. Forever grateful for all the help I received, I continued to work for the company for four more years. I had envisioned to expand the company into a meat-and-sausage-making operation and presented my proposal to the partners. It would require the company to invest in the equipment to produce smoked hams, kielbasa, bacon, and bologna, using the available empty spaces of the building. After initially agreeing, but later *renegging*, I realized there was too much WWII history to overcome and my vision would not ever happen, the new partner, also a Holocaust survivor like Wilbert, could not bring himself to rely on a German for the manufacturing venture, so he then withdrew his support. He apologized to me twenty-five years later at the funeral of our partner, Wilbert, that it was a mistake for him to deny me that opportunity. I reassured him that I never for a moment harbored any hard feelings toward him and that I was grateful for the time we did business together. "God works all things for the good for those who love him" (Rom. 8:28).

God Closes One Door and Opens Another Door!

A new opportunity presented itself to me when the owner of a building, leased to a German sausage-making operation in Meriden, Connecticut, tried to convince me to buy out either one or both partners presently leasing his building. If I agreed, he would terminate their lease agreement. This situation made the purchase of the company more affordable. After much prayer and consideration, I did pursue the offer, and after a year of negotiating, I was able to purchase the company with a partner. Twelve years earlier, I tried to buy the company with another partner but failed. God, in His infinite wisdom, knew I was not prepared and in need more training, which I did receive from the owner of the meat company I worked for at the time.

This was another one of those many God instances I could not shake off as good fortune, to finally own a USDA-approved sausage manufacturing business with a new partner, which we operated the company successfully for twenty-seven years.

11

HEALTH ISSUE

Two years before I purchased the sausage company, I experienced difficulties; while driving, I was unable to stay awake, and quite a few times, I woke up just before hitting another car. Or I unconsciously shifted lanes while driving and was not sure why I was driving in another lane and kept wondering what was happening to me. One morning, I was driving on a four-lane highway, when suddenly, my car spun out of control, crossing lanes several times, and finally headed over the embankment, coming to rest on top of a construction water culvert. By the grace of God, not being hurt but shaken up, I was still well enough to crawl back up to the highway, trying to catch the attention of passing cars. But to no avail; no one would stop. I walked to a nearby department store to call Roswitha to pick me up. Luckily, there was not too much damage, and after a tow truck pulled the car up to the street, we drove the car home with just a few dents in it. After that incident, I knew I needed medical attention, so I called my family doctor, who after the first examination, suspected a brain tumor or a severe case of hepatitis. He admitted me to the UConn Health Clinic for tests. After all tests came back inconclusive, I was sent home. But still unable to drive safely, it necessitated Roswitha to drive me to work and pick me up at the end of the day. Then on top of that, I could no longer safely keep boning beef, and after several deep cuts to my fingers, I performed other tasks that did not require a knife. Now, I was seriously thinking whether to continue to pursue the offer to buy out the partnership of the sausage-making company, but also realistically knew in my heart that I would not be able to debone beef much longer.

In the spring of 1983, I felt this strong urge to visit my mom in Germany and acted on it, taking my youngest daughter Ursula to see her grandmother, and I am forever grateful we did. My mother passed away two days later after our return. At the same time, I was also dealing with spiritual issues, when Ursula was denied her first communion rite in the Catholic church, which created in me a firestorm of anger toward the parish priest. But at the same time, it reawakened in me a desire to nourish my spiritual life, and my anger was directed more at myself than the priest who kept my little girl from the sacrament of Holy Communion. It was God's way to get my attention, and He sure did. We left our parish and joined another parish, where the priest welcomed our youngest daughter to receive her first communion. This incidence on top of my precarious health situation triggered in me an "aha" moment, recognizing that my faith had become too shallow, and that I needed to practice my faith in word and in deed.

I am tempted to call it a reawakening of my spiritual side that was always in me but had become lukewarm. From there on, we attended church regularly. But because of the purchase of the company in Meriden, Connecticut, it also necessitated moving closer to the new venture, and we moved to Cromwell, Connecticut. Once settled in Cromwell, we joined the parish of St. John's and actively took part in parish life, and with an added incentive for the sake of Sandra, Russell, Thomas, and Kathy who expressed a desire to be married in St. John's Catholic Church. Sandra and Russ married at St. John's on January 9, 1988, and later the same year on October 6, Thomas and Kathy also married at St. John's, and Fr. McGrath officiated at both weddings. Fr. McGrath was not the kind of priest we could easy warm-up to or enjoy like we did Fr. White. Roswitha tried to serve in a volunteer capacity in spiritual care of the parish but found too many hoops to jump through before she could serve in this role, and she stopped attending Mass. I continued to attend Mass and sing in the choir until Fr. McGrath dismissed the choir director, and the choir disbanded. Not one to want to miss singing in a choir, I joined the choir at First Congregational Church, and as I became more familiar with their worship service, it seemed that this was another puzzle in God's plan for me.

12

FAITH AND WORSHIP

God sent us an angel to guide us in our spiritual faith journey.
We were invited to attend the wedding of our friend's son in Denver, Colorado, and we became aware of the groom's sister's divorce and the struggle she experienced. Being our goddaughter, we invited her to come and live with us in Connecticut to gain some distance from her present circumstances. We were not expecting that she would take us up on the offer but not long after we received a call from our youngest daughter Ursula that a lady moved into our house. We did not expect that she would come to live with us. Barbara had become a "newborn Christian" and urged us to become "newborn Christians" also. Roswitha and I were Catholic, and our house guest Barbara insisted we must be saved, or we will end up in hell. Our understanding of how getting into heaven was somewhat different than her point of view, but we listened politely. After she found a Congregational church, she invited us to take part in a program she was to conduct, "Experiencing God," and experiencing God we did. In all my years, growing up in the Catholic faith, I never took part or contemplated joining a Bible study in a protestant church. One of the participants asked me if I would be willing to join a group of volunteers that visits youth offenders in prison, and for the life of me, I could not understand why I committed to minister to youth offenders two Sundays a month for two hours, driving

30 miles each way to the youth incarceration facility. I can only credit the Holy Spirit working in me!

Thinking back to that first Sunday at the youth prison, with a group of people I hardly knew, I was not sure what to say or how to interact with youth offenders, but heavily depending on the Holy Spirit to lead and guide me. Coming home after my first visit in the youth prison, and sharing with Roswitha what I experienced that day, she at once requested another application so she could join too. Once we both were vetted and approved, we served at Manson Youth Institution for the next ten years. God does work in mysterious ways. The Hound of Heaven continuously pursues those who are open to His calling.

Joining a Homeless Mission

Serving with a Protestant group, after joining a Congregational church, and the pastor approached us to ask if we would feel comfortable in joining a group of people from his church on a homeless mission, handing out sandwiches and blankets to the homeless living on the street in New York City. We thought this should be easy, but little did we know what was awaiting us. When the day for departure came, all the people from church backed out at the last moment. On our way to New York City, we contemplated to turn around but continued to the NYSUM mission house, which was cramped with people. The moment we stepped in and were signed in, we were ordered to head to the kitchen to cook and serve the other participants who came from all over America to serve the homeless. Doubting our ability to serve in this role, and not yet convinced we were meant to be there, we kept our eyes open for an opportunity to sneak out and head back to Connecticut. But rejections of assignments were not allowed, so we stayed. Later that first evening, and after two hours of instructions, we were on our way to go out on the street to minister to those laying on the sidewalk or sleeping in a cardboard box. We prayed and handed out toiletries, sandwiches, and blankets. What I saw was beyond what I could have imagined or could bear. Mothers and fathers clutching their little babies wrapped in blankets, hiding them from the authorities. Toddlers with their lips blue from shivering in zero temperature or sleeping in cardboard boxes. The next evening out on the street, we noticed two young human beings. We were not sure of their gender, but in danger of freezing to death on the sidewalk right in front of Central Railroad station. We suspected they were high on drugs since they were not coherent enough to seek shelter inside the train station entrance only thirty feet away. It felt like ten below zero that night. My partner and I approached the police officer to allow us to bring the two in and bed them down on an empty bench. We then continued to walk the streets until our supplies of sandwiches and blankets ran out at 3:00 a.m. Once back at the mission house, where the other volunteers already were praying and crying, never expecting to see human beings lying on cold pavements in cardboard boxes in subfreezing temperatures.

Another "Aha" Moment out on the Streets on Manhattan

The next night out again on the streets handing out sandwiches and blankets, Roswitha and I looked up and recognized the street's name. It was this same street we stood on thirty-two years earlier, after we disembarked from the SS *Maasdam*, and not sure where we would find shelter. At that moment, we realized how much our heavenly Father had provided, protected, and guided us then, and all the years since then. We fell into each other's arms and cried. The following morning, again we were assigned to prepare breakfast, but this time with a couple from Albany, New York. And joining them for breakfast, we saw a serene love emanating from that couple, so intense that we instinctively knew this was the kind of love we want for us. Later that night, we happened to be paired again to go out on the street handing out blankets, sandwiches, toiletries, and knocking on cardboard boxes, the homes of homeless. The cardboard boxes served to shelter them for the freezing temperatures. We were privileged to see this couple's compassion for the residents in those cardboard boxes. Being privy to how they were filled with compassion and embraced the homeless with their quiet love again has transformed Roswitha's and my life. Before returning home, all those at the mission house attended a charismatic Pentecostal worship service. The Times Square church was filled with street people, trying to hold on to their few belongings while worshipping, holding hands with ladies in fur coats. The singing and worshipping seemed to go on for an eternity. We returned to the mission house for lunch, and after lunch, we drove back to Connecticut, traumatized by what we had seen and experienced. We felt compelled to call our pastor for an appointment the next day.

13

RESISTANCE AND REJECTION

After ministering to the homeless in New York, driving back to Connecticut and completely overwhelmed by what we saw, we were eager to share what we experienced with our children. But to our surprise, we sensed adverse reactions. We raised our children in the Catholic faith and assumed they would be aware of the Lord's teaching from the Gospel of Matthew 25:35–36, "For I was hungry, and you gave me something to eat, I was thirsty, and you gave me something to drink, I was a stranger and you invited me. I needed clothes and you clothed me, I was sick, and you looked after me. I was in prison, and you came to visit me." Reaching out to the homeless on the streets of Manhattan was for us a life-changing experience. It reawakened our commitment to live our faith and to love unconditionally. Our faith made it possible for us to love our children regardless of their uneasiness of our newfound life serving in spiritual care ministries. Progressing to volunteering in convalescent homes, prisons, and hospitals may have added to their consternation and apprehension. But on the plus side, it fills our retirement years with a purpose and a mission.

SECTION 3

Post-Retirement

14

GROWING IN FAITH: JOSEF'S CONTINUING SPIRITUAL JOURNEY

However, it is written: "What no eye has seen, what no ear has heard, and what no human mind has conceived"—the things God has prepared for those who love him. Someone quipped, to love the saints up in heaven above, that will be glory, but to love the saints here below, that is a whole other story! But the Lord Jesus commanded us to love our neighbor as our self! (1 Cor. 2:9)

A new command I give you: *Love one another*. As I have loved you, so you must love one another. By this everyone will know that you are my disciples if you love one another. (John 13:34–35)

Keep on loving one another as brothers and sisters. Do not forget to show hospitality to strangers, for by so doing some people have

shown hospitality to angels without knowing it.
(Heb. 13:1–2)

There are many poor people in need today, not solely for lack of money, but a lack of hope and faith, and where there is no faith, there is a lack of hope, material wealth has the propensity to evaporate in the blink of an eye as millions of people experienced in 1929 and in 2008, when the real estate and the stock market collapsed and desperate people by the thousands jumped from their office windows to their deaths because their empires collapsed.

Who can imagine what God has in store for you when you fall in love head over heels with Jesus? I am a living testimony what God can do. After successfully running the company already for twenty-five years while also volunteering in prison and church ministries, was daunting at times, and I came to realize I had to pursue the sale of the company, to serve the Lord in whatever capacity the Lord had in store for me, with the energy still left in me, and where I can help others? We continued to serve at the mission house in New York twice a year for another four years until the administrators raised the fees higher than those willing to serve could afford, and when the church was not subsidizing the mission trips, the trips were ended. At that point in my journey of faith, I was eager to find a mission closer to home, I inquired at the Vincent de Paul Soup Kitchen near my home if I could be the chief dishwasher on Mondays when my shop was closed. Washing dishes, serving, and retrieving trays provided me the opportunities to engage with the guests in conversations while they were lining up to the counter to receive their food, or I would join them while eating my lunch. Looking for ways to reignite and expand my home church outreach ministry, I approached Sister Anne who was in charge if to ask if it would be possible for my church to serve two Sunday meals a year at Vincent DePaul's and she at once assigned my church to serve Easter dinner and another Sunday in the fall. The church has made it into tradition and is still fifteen years later serving two Sundays a year.

The Alpha Program

Our goddaughter, while still living in our house, became more active in her new church and signed us up to take participate in the Alpha program, designed to teach the basics of the Christian faith in thirteen weeks. Each session began with sharing a meal with assigned group members, engaging in conversation just getting to know each other. After dinner, followed by singing praise and worship songs, then followed a forty-minute video presentation and group discussions until the end of the session. It is described by its organizers as "an opportunity to explore the meaning of life." Alpha courses are hosted by churches, homes, workplaces, prisons, and a wide variety of other locations.

I can only surmise that Barbara, the one who made a nuisance of herself after moving into our home, who begged us to take part in the Alpha Program at her church. I was not so sure why I should be there, or what will come of it, and where it will lead me, but my heart miraculously was opened, and the Holy Spirit guided me. Admittedly, the idea of sharing, group singing, and openly praying together, not by rote, was not what I learned in the Catholic tradition and made me uncomfortable at first. It crossed my mind a few times not to return the following week, but soon, we made friends and could not imagine being without them. The next session of the alpha program, we were asked to be group leaders. Opening in prayer and say a closing prayer was for many participants as it was for me a sticky issue, and a few participants withdrew from the course. We then stopped asking new participants to open or close in prayer, unless we had approached them privately before the session to ask if they would want to do so. Alpha inspired me to rise every morning at 4:30 a.m. to read Scripture and learn to pray from the heart and have an intimate quiet time with my Lord.

Reading *The Interior Castle*, written by Theresa of Avila five hundred years earlier, was exactly the remedy to cure me of my deficient prayer life. From that time on, even when I was on the road for business, or driving alone in the car with the radio off, I engaged in lively conversations with my God. I soon came to realize that I did not have a personal relationship with my Lord Jesus for most of my life. I had religion, but no intimate relationship with my Lord. It saddens me when I think of all the time I lost by not having had those heart-to-heart talks with my God all those years. Good News, I found Jesus. No, He found me and led me in a new direction, a new life in Christ, with a new vision and a new mission for my life. Praying not just in the quiet time in the morning, but much of the day, often not realizing that there were other people within earshot, assuming this guy is talking to himself. The Holy Spirit revealed to me the real meaning of Jeremiah 29:13–15, "'Then you will call on me and come and pray to me, and I will listen to you. You will seek me and find me when you seek me with all your heart. I will be found by you,' declares the LORD, 'and will bring you back from captivity.'"

My captivity had a lot to do with the necessity of providing and raising my family. Being a husband, father, provider in a strange land, with strange customs and a different language and culture. To be successful in business demanded much of my energy. My waking hours were spent working six days every week to support the family, assuring the survival and success of the company.

Discerning: Have I loved the Lord with all my heart, or have I allowed too many other things to crowd out the Lord out? Especially those Sundays sleeping past church time to catch up on sleep. Many Sundays were reserved to take the family skiing, spending so-called quality time with our children in an activity we all enjoyed and being together the entire day. Many years had passed before we gravitated back to our spiritual roots, attending mass on Saturday evening or Sunday morning and taking part in church activities. Listening in a Mass to a homily about loving our neighbors as ourselves and love one another as I have loved you, I realized the Lord is asking me to not just to love Him, but to love one another as Jesus loved us.

Prison Alpha Ministry

When Connecticut Prison Alpha Program was organized, Roswitha and I were asked to introduce the alpha program in

Connecticut Penal Institutions in 1999, and since then, thousands of inmates have gained a new lease on life. Prison ministry can pose a challenge for anyone, especially once inside and you hear heavy iron doors slamming behind you, hearing the screaming of guards and German shepherds barking at the inmates, and still, you muster enough courage to follow the guards to their assigned classroom. Next, to hear the chatter and the footsteps of the offenders approaching the classroom to attend the session, and after recording their attendance, the officers leave and lock the door behind them. That is the moment when the rubber hits the road! It requires a love and compassion to love all inmates, no matter their appearance. There were volunteers who were unable to overcome their fears and doubts about spending time with convicts and sought safer venues to serve. There is also the widespread adage that convicts become *jailhouse Christians*, but I firmly believe that the Word is more powerful than a two-edged sword and can pierce even the hardest of hearts and souls. The fact is that almost all the volunteers have served faithfully already for fifteen years and continue to give of their time to share the gospel with incarcerated souls, a feat only God can do. Paul wrote in 1 Corinthians 3:6–11, "I planted the seed, Apollos watered it, but God makes it grow. So neither the one who plants nor the one who waters are anything, but only God, who makes things grow." With that in mind, I personally have never questioned or struggled with those dark moments that St. John of the Cross and Mother Therese of Kolkata (Calcutta) wrote about, questioning, "Why am I doing this?" But there were times when I felt death tired, and on my way to the prison, I prayed fervently to the Holy Spirit to give me the strength to conduct the sessions, and it never failed to rejuvenate me. Jackie Pullinger, a missionary in Hong Kong for thirty-five years, prayed, "Lord, give me a soft heart and hard feet." Or as Therese of Avila reminded the people of her day, that we are the hands and feet of our Lord Jesus on this earth. The Lord has a mission for everyone. In the Old Testament, He asked, "'Whom shall I send, and who will go for us?' Then said, 'Here am I; send me'" (Isa. 6:8–12). He needed a messenger, and He was asking who is willing. I have found encouragement and strength by studying the prophets of the

Old Testament, and the early church fathers and saints who had put their faith into action. For many years, I lacked the knowledge and understanding of why we need the saints as role models to focus on and what can we learn from them. They were ordinary people from different countries, cultures, and different languages and backgrounds. God will use all His children for His purpose, but like John the Baptist or Mary the mother of God who said, "I am the handmaiden of the Lord, be it to me as thou have said." This passage in the Gospel of Luke has been for me the pivotal verse in how I want to serve my Lord. When an opportunity presents itself, my worries mysteriously dissipate, and I am reminded from Philippians 4:13, "I can do all things through Him who gives me the strength."

I can only explain these moments by way of sharing my experiences out on the streets of Harlem doing homeless ministry or embracing my incarcerated brothers, reassuring them that God is right there in their midst. "For where two or three are gathered in my name, there am I in your midst" (Matt. 18:20). When I stand before a hospital room, I pray that the Lord will give me the words and the patience of a saint because I am not, and I rely on the Holy Spirit to help me. Now ministering at the state mental institution to patients, many of which are afflicted with mental illnesses, present an even bigger challenge. Remembering Roswitha and my first time serving the homeless out on the streets of New York was also a big challenge for both of us, and completely at a loss for words and quite numb at times, but with the power of His love and the Holy Spirit, we were empowered to stay and be the hands and feet of our Lord. Something came over us at that moment that I could never sufficiently explain. Every person we met on the sidewalks of Manhattan or the Bronx, whether walking or sleeping in cardboard boxes on subway shaft grids to keep from freezing to death, or desperately in need of an embrace, we just felt empowered to embrace them, hand them a blanket and a sandwich, and offered to pray for and with them.

I have never been confronted with that kind of destitution, but at the same time, love was flowing freely between us despite our differences in ethnicity, lifestyle, color. It all dissipated in seconds, and we bonded instantly as brothers and sisters. For Roswitha and me, this mission outreach has opened our eyes in ways we could never have imagined, and we knew from that moment on we could never walk by a person that is hurting and fail to minister to those in need or act like the priest and the Levite did. In Luke 10:30–34, Jesus said,

> A man was going down from Jerusalem to Jericho, when he was attacked by robbers. They stripped him of his clothes, beat him and went away, leaving him half dead. A priest happened to be going down the same road, and when he saw the man, he passed by on the other side. So too, a Levite, when he came to the place and saw him, passed by on the other side. But a Samaritan, as he traveled, came where the man was; and when he saw him, he took pity on him. He went to him and bandaged his wounds, pouring on oil and wine. Then he put the man on his own donkey, brought him to an inn and took care of him.

One day, while ministering to the homeless, we happened to stand on the same street we had stood on thirty-six years earlier and did not know where we will find shelter. We fell into each other's arms and cried because of the realization of how much our Lord has been there with us every step of the way. From there on, our desire to be in a closer relationship with Jesus deepened and is still growing, going to church feeling His presence and communicating with God and soaking in more of Jesus. St. Augustin so aptly pointed out when he wrote, "Thou hast made us for thyself, O Lord, and our heart is restless until it finds rest in thee." And we found that peace that surpasses all our understanding that only the Lord Jesus could give us. I knew there was no turning back to my old ways, and with whom I wanted to spend my time. I am persuaded that if you close a door behind you for the Lord, He opens many other doors ahead for you. Someone wrote the words to a song, "The world behind me, no turning back, no turning back." It became so real to me. I just knew in my heart that it would just be the beginning. I began to read more of the sacred Scriptures, using every trick in the book to memorize and retain and understand the reading what it means what Jesus promised His disciples before He rose to heaven, that "I will not leave you orphans, I will send you a counselor, a comforter." How reassuring and comforting for me that the Holy Spirit will be guiding me. I knew that I knew that wherever He leads me, He will also equip me. Someone wrote, and I quote, "God, does not only call the qualified, but he will qualify those He calls."

Now, that I am in my later years and my mind is not as sharp as it used to be, when writing my outlines for the messages I share, sometimes one or two in a week, I pray and ask God to lead me. When I am sharing a message, I focus on those listening to the word I share. What joy to see the power of the Word penetrating the hard shells some patients have enveloped themselves with. Whenever I am about to enter a hospital room, I pause for a few seconds and ask the Lord to take away any apprehension about what to say to the patient, and then, even difficult patients loosen up and open their hearts. There are patients now and then who will not allow me to share a prayer or engage in a conversation, especially while still partially sedated, or simply, they are not ready yet to accept a prayer.

The rich young ruler who asked the Lord what he needs to do to gain entrance to the kingdom of heaven, he was not ready either, and walked away, and Jesus did not run after him. This was an important lesson for me to learn, to shake the dust of my feet and go and bless someone else. We cannot argue anyone into heaven, even Jesus did not do well with that, and not everyone was open and followed Him. In my evangelistic approaches, I take heed how Jesus approached the woman at the well in John 4. As I recall, Jesus asked the woman for a drink of water and, later in their conversation, offered the woman living water, but it was still her choice to run into town and tell everyone who she met at the well, who told her things that only God could have known.

In the ministries I am privileged to serve, these two passages often come to my mind, and I realize I can never be an enforcer. I am just a messenger, and it is entirely in His hand what will happen. I am so grateful that the Lord instilled in me the desire to go wherever He sends me. St. Francis prayed, "Lord, make me an instrument of your peace, let me comfort those who need to be comforted, and console, not to be consoled." When we minister, whether it is in prison or a hospital, it is there that the Lord fine tunes His servants, just like the apostles when they were sharing their God-given talents to advance the Kingdom of God. I came to a point in my life when I realized that faithfully attending church on Sunday mornings, and by rote, repeat the prayers we all learned already as children, it will not produce the spiritual worship the Lord had in mind for His followers.

The spiritual nourishment of a homily and gather in the name of Jesus is all important, but Jesus said, "Then go out into all the world and make disciples of all nations," which in today's secular culture can make us very uncomfortable, and most likely was for His disciples too. Jesus commanded them, "Now go out into all the world and baptize in the name of the Father, the Son, and the Holy Ghost." The day the Lord put it on my heart to go to minister to the youths in prison and then to the maximum prison with the metal doors clonking behind me, I could not help but thinking of Daniel in the lion's den but knew that Daniel was not alone, the Lord was right there besides him and shutting the lion's mouths.

Geriatric Chaplain Ministry: A New Mission

One morning in 2008, while sitting at the breakfast reading the Meriden Record Journal, I happened to notice an ad seeking volunteers who would commit to eight weeks of chaplain geriatric pastoral care training, and in upon completion serve four hours a week for one year as a chaplain volunteer at the Masonic Care Center in Wallingford, Connecticut. Since I was already contemplating retirement, considering what I would do with my time when the moment came, I cut out the ad and brought it home and showed it to Roswitha. We decided to contact the spiritual director of the Masonic Home who instructed us to draft an essay about our life, why we wanted to serve as pastoral care volunteers in a geriatric long-term care facility. And completing the application, and after a successful interview, and completing the training course, were commissioned to begin our mission. I chalk it up to just another one of those God moments, to be privileged to serve Christ by visiting and comforting residents in this Alzheimer long-term-care facility. The training has equipped both of us with the necessary skills to comfort the residents, who feel abandoned by their families, many suffering the loss of their memory, their independence, their friends, and their homes.

This new mission was in preparation for the new purposes God had in store for me since I was already contemplating retirement and looking for ways to serve in whatever purpose or activity pleased the Lord after selling the company. As in so many cases before, faith again playing a role, in alerting me to that small ad in the local paper seeking volunteers to give to eight weeks of chaplain care training, to pastoral care for geriatric and Alzheimer patients. I would choose this program as the foundation of our commitment to devote the rest of our lives to pastoral care ministry. After two more years searching for a buyer, the sale of the company was finally brought to a successful conclusion. Now, finally free from the daily burden of working six days a week, which has been my lot for fifty-four years, I felt free to contact Middlesex Hospital to see if there was an opening for two volunteer positions. We completed and passed the mandatory training and health examinations. The hospital informed us that we would officially be joining the hospital pastoral care team.

Hospital Pastoral Care

Recalling my first visit in the Alzheimer ward, when our head chaplain assigned ten rooms to each volunteer chaplain with two residents in each room, and I was trembling and searching for words to say, but at that moment was reminded by the Holy Spirit of the words our Lord Jesus said to His disciples in the book of Luke, "When you are brought before synagogues, rulers and authorities, do not worry about how you will defend yourselves or what you will say, for the Holy Spirit will teach you at that time what you should say." Different condition, but reassured, that we can do all things through him who gives us the strength to go in and minister to whosoever

I will meet (Phil. 4:13). As an ecumenical pastoral care volunteer, we are called to serve Holy Communion to Catholic patients, and Protestant patients as part of pastoral care. Roswitha and I, at that time, still serving as deacons in a congregational church, caused me to scratch my head. *What else had the Lord in store for me?* But the words of Theresa of Calcutta comforted me; she wrote, "God does not ask you to be successful, but to be faithful." Paul's letter to the Ephesians 4:3–6 states,

> As a prisoner for the LORD, then, I urge you to live a life worthy of the calling you have received. Be completely humble and gentle; be patient, bearing with one another in love. Make every effort to keep the unity of the Spirit through the bond of peace. There is one body and one Spirit, just as you were called to one hope when you were called; one LORD, one faith, one baptism; one God and Father of all, who is over all and through all and in all.

Ever since I pledged my life to the Lord, living as prisoner of the Lord sounded so true, I knew, I could never back out, and the only solution for me was to trust Him and not lean on my own understanding. The Lord never fails to send angels at the right time and the right place, especially when we are doubting our ability. The Lord did send us an experienced spiritual care director, a Franciscan of the third order (lay Franciscans), who mentored us in all aspects of chaplain ministry. Considering again what Paul wrote in 1 Corinthians 2:9, "However, as it is written: 'What no eye has seen, what no ear has heard, and what no human mind has conceived,'" the things God has prepared for those who love him. The Lord must have felt assured that we love Him very much. Roswitha and I had both grown up in the Catholic faith but have moved on to attend a congregational church and had already been serving as deacons in that nondenominational church for a number of years and now being asked to bring communion to Catholic patients, seemed to me like a big obstacle, but we were assured not to worry, as the head chaplain, a Franciscan of the Third Order, ecumenically minded explained to us that he wanted us to comfort and pray with all patients, regardless of their denominations, and the gratitude and love we experienced uniformly from patients of all faiths goes beyond what I ever had experienced before.

Mental Hospital Chaplaincy Ministry

Within weeks after we have been accepted to the hospital care team, I also received a call from the spiritual director of Connecticut Valley Hospital, asking me if I would come and minister to mental health and detox patients. I had reservations about my ability to ministering to mental patients, which would be a first for me. I have been ministering to inmates in youth prison and hardened criminals, but to share the Gospel to mentally challenged patients? I was not so sure. Recalling Paul's word to the Corinthians: "However, as it is written: 'What no eye has seen, what no ear has heard and what no human mind has conceived' the things God has prepared for those who love him" (1 Cor. 2:9 NIV). To present the Good News in such a way that the patients hear the message but not harm themselves by the content of the message. There has been one instance where a patient, after hearing Mark 9:47: "And if your eye causes you to stumble, pluck it out. It is better for you to enter the kingdom of God with one eye than to have two eyes, and thrown into hell, and acted on it, and is now blind in both eyes." As if this were not yet challenging enough, one year later, I was asked, if I would conduct a Christian worship service at Whiting Forensic Institute for the Criminal Insane, housing patients who committed heinous crimes and pleaded insane offense. Now ten years later, and looking back, it is a real-life miracle to share the Good News without any incidents or disciplinary incidents.

Discovering the True Meaning of a Life in Christ Jesus

My life in Christ has opened my eyes to the fact that it was not the Catholic church, which did not properly prepare me for my journey in the Lord, but it was I who has been the laggard, who had shortchanged my faith. If I had read scriptures and earnestly looked for and received the sacraments regularly with all my heart, mind, soul, and strength, then I would not have spent all those years, being a lukewarm Catholic. The good news, God never stopped sending angels my way because of His unconditional love, even when I was oblivious to the fact that God did send all those angels my way. My mother was one of those caring angels; when strangers in need who showed up at her door, she invited them into her home and shared a meal, and often also offered them shelter. "Do not forget to entertain strangers, for by so doing some people have entertained angels" (Heb. 13:1). God works in mysterious ways; when our goddaughter Barbara showed up unannounced and in need of a home to recuperate from her disastrous marriage, she came to live with us. She was a very strange angel indeed, making a nuisance of herself by telling us that we will end up in hell if we do not accept Jesus Christ as our Lord and Savior. Roswitha and I, both Catholic all our lives, and our new house guest had the nerve to haul us to a Protestant church where she was leading a Bible study and then signed us up to an Alpha Course. How can I explain the how and why we allowed it to happen? Now there was no turning back, even at the cost of losing friends and the displeasure of our children. True to the words of the hymn, "I have decided to follow Jesus; The world behind me, the cross before me. Though none go with me, still I will follow; No turning back; no turning back" (S. Sundar Singh, "I Have Decided to Follow Jesus"). This was so true for us, as we looked forward no matter the cost.

> Do not suppose that I have come to bring peace to the earth. I did not come to bring peace, but a sword. For I have come to turn "a man against his father, a daughter against her mother,

a daughter-in-law against her mother-in-law a man's enemies will be the members of his own household." Anyone who loves their father or mother more than me is not worthy of me; anyone who loves their son or daughter more than me is not worthy of me. Whoever does not take up their cross and follow me is not worthy of me. Whoever finds their life will lose it, and whoever loses their life for my sake will find it. (Matt. 10:34–39)

We did not expect the kind of opposition we encountered from our children, but our new life in Christ is all worth it, as it has given us a life so rich that nothing could compare with our new life in Christ Jesus. Paul tells it so well: "Whatsoever was to my profit I now consider rubbish compared to the life in Christ Jesus my Lord" (Phil. 3:7–14).

The Lord increased my assignments in all places I was invited to share a message, and my desire to learn and understand and apply Scripture in my life became so overwhelming that to satisfy my hunger and thirst for His Word, I began to rise at 4:30 a.m. every morning to intimately communicate with my Lord and read Scripture to equip me for the day ahead. Writing my sermon outlines without interruptions, in quiet time meditate on the scripture passage I had chosen for the services of that week. How many times have I prayed like Jabez prayed in 1 Chronicles 4: 10. "Jabez cried out to the God of Israel, 'Oh, that you would bless me indeed, and enlarge my territory! Let your hand be with me and cause no harm and keep me from harm so that I will be free from pain.'" And God granted his request, but God also did bring me pain, like Paul's thorn in his flesh to keep him from becoming conceited. Losing many friends and not being welcomed anymore in the ethnic social club we belonged to but knowing that I could not in good conscience espouse or embrace or belong to anymore.

Looking back, it was these rejections that inspired me to press on even more: "Brothers and sisters, I do not consider myself yet to have taken hold of it. But one thing I do: Forgetting what is behind and straining toward what is ahead, I press on toward the goal to win the prize for which God has called me heavenward in Christ Jesus" (Phil. 3:13–14).

Participating in Bible studies, prayer breakfasts, and youth offender ministry has offered me opportunities beyond my wildest dreams and privileged to lead many young inmates to Christ Jesus, from which they had separated themselves and fallen to the evil's schemes as the Lord Jesus told the people in the days when our Lord walked the earth: "I have come to give life, the evil one is a liar from day one and only comes to kill and destroy." I can vouch how successfully evil destroys beautiful young men who followed him down the road to incarceration and separation from their families, and now trying to wrest them away from the evil's clutches. Changes are sometimes very radical or may develop over time. In my case, at first, I noticed minor changes in me. I lost the desire to impress friends with my ability to remember jokes, not all of them clean enough to share in the presence of people of faith. There also was an increasing need to be nourished by the Word. "As the deer panted for the water, so my soul panted after thee" (Ps. 42:1). And little by little, the intensity to seek the Word, and how I saw people now as Christ would see them increased, and I felt like Paul speaks of in Philippians 1:21, "For to me, to live is Christ and to die is gain." I died to myself but gained a whole new life when I asked the Lord for more of Him in my life, and make me as thirsty as David when he was in the desert (Ps. 42).

15

THEOLOGY AND HISTORY

Challenging the New World Order

In 2012, I was invited to study with the Colson Centurion program to be a Colson fellow. After completing the one-year course, now renamed Colson Fellowship, which I am now a mentor for the new students, who come from all social classes, many of whom are in their later years, and mature Christian backgrounds. Chuck Colson, the infamous White House lawyer for President Richard Nixon, who engaged in questionable practices that forced the resignation of Richard Nixon from the presidency. Chuck Colson was sentenced to six years in federal penitentiary for his crime. While incarcerated, he was evangelized, and after his release, founded Prison Fellowship. Chuck Colson was instrumental in the establishment of the Centurion Program for the purpose of marshaling Christians to defend a Christian worldview versus a secular worldview.

At the time I was invited to become a Centurion, I already served as a chaplain volunteer in hospitals and prisons and been aware of the fallout that lives lived without biblical precepts can lead to. I felt called to get involved in the battle to change a culture that is moving away at warped speed from Christian ethics and morals. Praying to the Holy Spirit to lead me in the direction where I can apply my newly gained knowledge and what role I can play to curb a culture that embraces abortion and euthanasia, same-sex marriage, and transgenderism. Part of the Centurion Program entails for participants to develop a three-year plan to educate people about a Christian worldview. I was already reaching more people by praying with mental patients and comforting the aged in my pastoral ministries and seeking ways to reach more people and felt drawn to write comments on social media to alert society of the consequences of a culture where morals and ethics are replaced with ruthless business practices and alternative lifestyles and Christian morality frowned upon.

The first book I wrote focuses on the breakup of the traditional family, demanding two breadwinners to keep the wolves from the door, which is triggering a multitude of problems for children, families, and communities and the whole nation. Inner-city high school dropout rates are increasing, not decreasing. Belligerent behaviors of young people are leading to too many of the young, especially males to be incarcerated and not able to start a family of their own. Federal and state reentry programs have had limited success in integrating offenders back into the community, proved by a recidivism rate of 80 percent, and a good sign that government programs alone cannot reduce the level of violence on the streets of New York, Chicago, or Los Angeles or any other city.

Not wanting to sound overly religious, but 2 Corinthians 5:16–21 is the roadmap for changing people: "So from now on we regard no one from a worldly point of view. Though we once regarded Christ in this way, we do so no longer. Therefore, if anyone is in Christ, he is a new creation, the old has gone, the new is here!" Why would a secular world experiencing mass shootings and unprecedented level of violence not wanting to reach for the life preserver that is freely available for anyone and everyone? "The Spirit and the bride say, 'Come.' And let the one who hears say, 'Come.' Let the one who is thirsty come; and let the one who wishes and take the gift of the water of life" (Rev. 22:17). Could it be that the popular secular culture is worshiping the other gods that Jesus warned us about, who lead us to destruction, but unable to admit that their "way" has not been a positive way but has utterly failed and has destroyed untold lives because of violence and crime? When the Lord Jesus begun His ministry here on earth, the temple authorities questioned the Lord about His mission. Jesus opened the scroll and began quoting Isaiah 61:1–3,

> The Spirit of the Sovereign LORD is on me, because the LORD has anointed me to proclaim good news to the poor. He has sent me to bind up the brokenhearted, to proclaim freedom for the captives and release from darkness for the prisoners, to proclaim the year of the LORD's favor and the day of vengeance of our God, to comfort all who mourn, and provide for those who grieve in Zion to bestow on them a crown of beauty instead of ashes, the oil of joy instead of mourning, and a garment of praise instead of a spirit of despair.

It was successful in 33 AD and has led from pagan practices, and they became followers of Christ, known as the people of the way! This sounds like a winning plan to me!

What Was the Pagan Way?

Sacrificing their children to placate their gods, crucifying criminals, and displaying their decomposing bodies to intimidate anyone opposing their rulers. Maintaining houses of male and female prostitution, discarding unwanted babies by leaving them unprotected out on the streets of Rome for animals to devour them. Infanticide was the root cause of contributing to the inability of Rome to defend itself against the invaders because of a lack of a homegrown army. Instead, they had to rely on pagan mercenaries, and once they grew in numbers, they became strong enough to overthrow the rulers that hired them. Some historians concluded that infanticide and the depraved culture was responsible for the decline and ruin of the Roman Empire. In the Americas, the Inca, Mayan, and Aztec empires worshipped gods who demanded warm human hearts, cut out of live young maidens and boys to placate their gods by the hundred thousand, and they sacrificed them on the altars of their gods. The Spaniards, who were not by any stretch of the imagination saints, introduced the natives to worship a god who did not demand the sacrifice of their children on their high altars anymore, as the Incas were doing, or pagans did in the Old Testament to the gods of Baal and Moloch.

Jesus repeatedly said, "I am the way, the truth, and the life," and it is one of the seven "I Am" statements of Jesus. He did not state there are some, or many other ways to get to heaven.

As a Christian and as a Centurion, with a deep love and concern for my fellow sojourners on this earth, I find it necessary to follow the model that describes the ministry of Jesus in (Isa. 61), He came to alleviate the pains and the suffering the secular culture heaped upon the suffering poor people of His days on earth day (61:1–2): "The Spirit of the Sovereign Lord is on me, because the Lord has anointed me to proclaim good news to the poor. He has sent me to bind up the brokenhearted, to proclaim freedom for the captives and release from darkness for the prisoners." I feel moved to let the Spirit of the Lord lead me to comfort those who are in need to be comforted and console, not so much to be consoled. Whether rich or poor human beings, their hearts and souls are troubled and cannot find the rest they so desperately need and seek, which only the Lord can give. St. Augustin of Hippo has said, "Thou hast made us for thyself, O Lord, and our hearts are restless until they find rest in thee."

God led me in so many positive directions, financially and spiritually, too many to mention them all. By God's providence, I was called to serve my God with all my heart and soul in all the ways the Lord would lead me. The disconnection from my responsibilities in managing the company allowed me to dedicate my time to where the Lord led me. "Now to him who can do immeasurably more than all we ask or imagine, according to his power that is at work within us" (Eph. 3:20). The Lord instilled in me the thirst and the desire to read Scriptures and daily prayer that I could never have imagined.

Celebrating my seventy-sixth birthday and keenly aware of the time clock of life but gratefully enjoying every moment the Lord provided, I had a burning desire to jump at every opportunity to draw more people to the Lord, and especially the prodigals who have fallen away. The Lord Jesus said, "The thief cometh not, but for to steal, and to kill, and to destroy, I am come that they might have life, and that they might have it more abundantly" (John 10:10). C. S. Lewis wrote *The Screw Tape Letters*, first published in February 1942. The story takes the form of a series of letters from a senior demon Screwtape to his nephew Wormwood, a Junior Tempter. The uncle's mentorship pertains to the nephew's responsibility in securing the damnation of a British man known only as "the Patient." Interspersed with observations on human nature in the Bible. Screwtape's advice for selfish gain and power are the only good, and neither demon can understand God's love for man or acknowledge human virtue. This describes the schemes the evil ones who uses every tool at his disposal to wrest humans away from the good plans the Lord has prepared for them.

Adam and Eve are poster children of the evil one's success in detaching the sheep from the Good Shepherd. Living a life without faith in God, the Lord Jesus, and the Holy Spirit is not a life worth living. Material wealth, fame, fortune, strength, and beauty can all be gone in the blink of an eye or fade away. Many have been chasing earthly riches all their lives but lack the most important ingredient, the joy of the Lord and the peace that only the Lord can provide. "If I have the gift of prophecy and can fathom all mysteries and all knowledge, and if I have a faith that can move mountains, but do not have love, we are nothing but an empty clanging cymbal" (1 Cor. 13:2). Johnny Lee sang, "I am looking in all the wrong places for love."

Isaiah 45:23 is a stark reminder of what awaits every human being at the end of the journey on this earth. In this passage, the Lord God vows that every person will bow before him. No gender, religion, race, or status will matter; all equally must stand before God and would like to hear the words from God: "His master replied, 'Well done my good and faithful servant! You have been faithful with a few things; I will put you in charge of many things. Come and share your master's happiness!" (Matt. 25:21).

Erma Bombeck wrote, and I quote, "At the end of my life, when I have to stand before God, I would hope that I have used all the talents the Lord has given me." This has been my guiding principle, making sure that I would not be wasting my God-given time and talents on endless TV or internet distractions. I am convinced that this is what the Lord has warned us about in John 10:10, "The Thief comes to kill and destroy," and it includes killing the time we have, instead of making a difference in someone's life. My love for Jesus exhorts me to resist the evil's plans, preventing me from reading the Holy Scriptures and the indwelling of His Word and not gaining the confidence to speak His Word and sharing His love in as many locations the Lord opened doors for me to walk through.

Can I proclaim to be a confessing Christian and fall in line with the prevailing culture of death, perpetuated by legalized abortion, which allows aborting eight hundred thousand babies, being dismembered in their mother's womb every year, even up to the moment of their birth, and celebrated as a freedom of choice.

> "Son of man, I have made you a watchman for the people of Israel; so, hear the word I speak and give them warning from me. When I say to a wicked person, 'You will surely die,' and you do not warn them or speak out to dissuade them from their evil ways to save their life, that wicked person will die for their sin, and I will hold you accountable for their blood. But if you do warn the wicked person and they do not turn from their wickedness or from their evil ways, they will die for their sin; but you will have saved yourself." (Ezek. 3:17–27 NIV)

One only must-read Eric Metaxas biography of Dietrich Bonhoeffer and Martin Niemöller, who both lamented that the German Catholic bishops and Protestant bishops were not speaking out forcefully enough about the catastrophe and what Nazism would have on Germany in their near future.

Studying world history and living the history of Germany, which I had the privilege of growing up in, but experiencing the horrible consequences caused by a godless regime, now I see a repeat of the same drift of policies that caused so much destruction of WWII, and it has led me, a professing believer, to speak up, wherever possible.

Speaking up and living a life devoted to God and His precepts is increasingly challenging in the prevailing atmosphere of the secular worldview environment here in the US. I have experienced drastic changes in the attitudes of my friends toward me and my wife. Soon after we gave our life to Christ, many of our associations cooled off to the point that we had to find more Christ-oriented friends, not always perfect, but more in line with the teaching of our Lord Jesus. Our own children, educated in public schools and colleges, were deluged in postmodern culture and not inclined to listen to their Bible-believing parents, who entrusted their lives in the Lord, instead of the popular culture of our day. The god of the postmodern culture is pluralism, popularism, and no absolutisms. Darwinism theory of creation and evolution cannot coexist with the biblical condemnation of worshipping other gods. "You shall have no other gods before me. God does not allow us to bow down to any other gods, but only worship the God of Abraham, Jacob, Isaac" (Exod. 20:1).

Generations Caught up in the Maelstrom of Darwinian Evolution Theory

Since 1930, five generations of public-school educated children have been exposed to in science classes to the teachings of Darwin's evolutionary teaching, but not in biblical precepts. Millennials, in large numbers, endorse abortion in all stages of gestation, and at the time of this writing, eleven states have enacted laws for doctor-aided euthanasia on demand. How far can it be when millennials will outnumber the gray panther voters in the ballot box, who, just a few years ago, dominated the outcome of elections but are now in the minority and rapidly declining? Visiting old-age and convalescence homes would make the millennial and Z generation more aware that they, too, will be one day in danger of being the subject of a meeting, whereby vote, it is decided whether the resources spent justify the means to keep grandma or grandpa breathing any longer. The word used to justify euthanasia is "quality of life," and Medicare, overburdened because of prohibitive expenditures, elect ethics committees who will then figure out if the expenditures are justified, and this by a government committee, not the patient's family when their parents' days on earth will be ended. Euthanasia has already been legalized in Belgium and the Netherlands for a few years.

I, being born in 1943, at the height of power of one of the most murderous dictatorships known in history, determined to cleanse the gene pool of any undesirable human beings (*Untermenschen*) contaminating the Aryan Race, chances could have meant that I could have been exterminated for any evidence of a mental or physical deformity, either obvious or just suspected. Those voicing objections to medically induced deaths are now, just as they were eighty years ago, shunned by their former friends and associates and labeled "deplorable fundamental Christian fanatics," or as in Germany, now labeled as "other thinkers." Having been born in a time when a Christian nation like Germany, with a 95 percent Christian population, equally divided between Catholics and Protestants, by their silence became active participants in the monstrous murder of the mentally challenged, the infirm, Gypsies, Jews and Slavish people, and after the war, vehemently denied any knowledge of the horrors, many claiming their innocence by being oblivious of the atrocities committed in twenty-three death camps, and nine hundred subcamps spread all over Germany and Poland. SS Death Brigades indiscriminately killed entire populations of villages from Lithuania, Ukraine, Russia, Slovakia, Hungary, all the way down to the Balkan Nations.

All these atrocities have affected me personally, especially being born in 1943, when marauding SS and the Gestapo dragged children from their German mothers' arms because they considered them not suited to propagate the ideal master race. I have visited the death camps in Dachau and Buchenwald, and I was horrified what human beings are capable of when successfully indoctrinated and brainwashed into a murderous ideology. I have previously authored a book, devoting one chapter about the killing of millions of babies in the US in the womb of their mothers, who by God's design, should be safe in their mothers' wombs. I am even more outraged and compelled to speak out as state governments have legalized the murdering of innocent children being murdered already out of the womb of the mother. When legislation was signed by the governor in Albany, New York, and women attending the signing were applauding and celebrating, it was reminiscent of Nazi leaders celebrating when innocent people were exterminated. This culture of death has reinforced my faith in the dignity of every human being to a life, liberty, and the pursuit of happiness, and increased my desire to speak out about this atrocity and work toward the restoration of Christian values.

The Irrationality of Darwinian Evolutionary Theory

Molecular scientists have proven Darwin's evolutionary theory as improbable, as creation needs a creator-designer of earth and humans but is not allowed to be taught in America's classrooms, which is reminiscent of what occurred in Nazi-era public schools. A good example is what occurred in Nazi-era public schools. Denys Louis de Rougemont was a Swiss writer and cultural theorist who wrote in French. One of the nonconformists of the 1930s, he addressed the perils of totalitarianism from a Christian point of view. De Rougemont recounted,

> They pointed out that only workers and peasants benefited from Nazi reforms, while their own values were being systematically destroyed by devious methods. They were taxed disproportionately, their family life had been irreparably harmed, parental authority sapped, religion stripped, and education eliminated.

A lawyer's wife complained to him, "Every evening, my two children are taken over by the Party." This experience was not particularly different from what was happening at the same time to the children of Soviet parents. The Nazis, being utopian fanatics, more concerned with the future than the present, were prepared to pay quite a high price for taking over the minds of the young. As Thomas Mann's daughter Erika pointed out in her excoriating book on the subject, "School for Barbarians," the quality of education was gravely damaged under the Hitler regime, which (as left-wing regimes also often do) promoted or protected bad but politically acceptable teachers and polluted the teaching of all arts and historical subjects. It believed it was more urgent to teach the young what to think than to show them how to think. Hitler himself taunted his opponents for their powerlessness against him.

They might rage at him as much as they liked, but "When an opponent declares 'I will not come over to your side' I say calmly 'Your child belongs to us already. What are you? You will pass on. Your descendants, however, now stand in the new camp. In a short time, they will know nothing but this new community.'" He was so right. This does reflect the power of a liberal educated elite in charge of institutions of higher learning practicing and teaching in the US today, and I agree, they learned from the best. Only the best did mislead a whole generation into marching to their deaths in the war that followed. History will repeat itself; only this time, the war is on Christianity. The elites are fighting to create a new society where sexual restraints are limited only to nonconsensual partners, but when consensual any combination can and will be made legal as same-sex partner marriages are already legalized in all states. In the span of forty years, the Christian worldview has been supplanted with a secular worldview that says evil is good, and good is evil, and natural laws can be exchanged for unnatural laws, and anything is possible. Suzy can be Gregory, and Max can be with a medical procedure be Sally, and only a seismic intervention by the Creator of this universe can bring this madness to screeching halt. Ancient biblical history has shown that God did intervene and allow catastrophic calamities to occur, so His people would call out to God to restore their nations. The cities of Sodom and Gomorrah were destroyed, and only Abraham's family and Lot survived.

The Designer Theory

The Christian worldview has been exchanged with a secular postmodern worldview without absolutes, rendering natural laws obsolete in the belief that the DNA and the natural order can be manipulated to change reproduction. Quoting Dr. Glenn Sunshine from his book *Portals*, "that the postmodern purpose is to create a world where everyone is free to live out her or his own self-defined identity, free of judgment from others, with all essential needs guaranteed and supplied by society." This idea that society must fund the necessary medical procedures to transition from male to female or female to male has recently been demonstrated by numerous court cases where members of the military are suing the armed forces who where up to now not willing to fund all costs involved in changing a soldiers natural identity. But now, it is legislated by states and federal authorities and enforced by the courts, causing to increase the burden on the taxpayers and insurance industry, and will increase premiums to astronomical heights. It will also require increases in the collection of Medicare payroll deductions. What this clearly proves is the difficulties associated with attempts to change the God-ordained natural order leading to very unnatural disruptions of the natural order of society.

The famous French philosopher and mathematician René Descartes (1596–1650), known as the father of modern philosophy, declared, "I think therefore I am." Much of his work tried to defy skepticism, a prominent ideology for the French intellectuals of the day. In addition, much of his philosophical thinking led him to speculate about the connection between the mind and the body, which is what this quote focuses upon. Descartes was dissatisfied with the scholastic philosophers of his time. He wanted a fresh look on philosophy and developed his own method of radical doubt. The cogito argument is what Descartes used as the basis of this method to discover whether our beliefs, were to be trusted, which led him to the conclusion "I think, therefore I am."

This seems to suggest that because I am a man in a woman's body or vice versa, I can transgender into a new identity. The problem with transgenderism begins with one of the most basics need of humanity, the call of nature to expel waste from the physical body when in public buildings and places and has been for centuries denoted as man or female bathrooms. The first sex-segregated toilet laws were set up in Paris in the 1700s. American men and women use of separate restrooms started in the late 1800s, when Massachusetts required separate privies in businesses. To stretch the imagination a little further, imagine a former female wanting to marry a former male and requesting a minister or priest to officiate in their marriage ceremony. If this seems to be a little farfetched, think again; think of all the unimaginable changes the culture has experienced in just the last fifty years. What was once thought impossible is now made possible by a society accepting the undoing of the natural order through the advances of medical science and psychiatric interventions and consultations.

Psychiatric and medical professionals have been the beneficiaries of these changes by way of securing an ever-increasing flow of revenue far into the future, as the changes cause continued medical attention and medications and psychiatric consultations. John Hopkins Hospital in Baltimore discontinued sex-change procedures in 1979. Once at the forefront of gender-identity science and site of the nation's first "change-of-sex operations," as the headlines announced in 1966—Hopkins abruptly halted those surgeries in 1979. The main trigger was a study by Jon Meyer, head of the hospital's Sexual Behaviors Consultation Unit. Johns Hopkins resumed gender-reassignment surgeries after thirty-eight-year hiatus.

McHugh, the hospital's chief of psychiatry from 1975 to 2001 still believes that being transgender is a psychological problem, not a biological phenomenon. And the University Distinguished Service Professor at Johns Hopkins Medicine, Dr. McHugh is often quoted on gender issues in conservative media. "I'm not against transgender people," he said recently, stressing that he is "anxious they get the help they need." But such help should be psychiatric rather than surgical, he supports.

Paul Rodney McHugh is a vocal proponent of Catholic-informed and socially conservative stances on issues on gender and sexuality, most notably expressed in a 2016 report he authored for *The New Atlantis*. The report received strong criticism from many scientists, researchers, and Johns Hopkins faculty who criticized McHugh for "misrepresenting" scientific evidence and "cherry-picking" data, noting that McHugh has done little scientific research in this area. Over six hundred faculty, researchers, and students at Johns Hopkins cosigned a letter condemning his report. Geneticist Dean Hamer expressed "disgust" that McHugh had "twisted and misrepresented" the work of scientists including himself. What it reveals is the power and influence the LGBTQA can exert over scientific proof to legitimize the unnatural and abrogate scientific research and Dr. McHugh was forced to resign.

Christian Moral, Values and Ethics

The suppression of conservative Christian speakers taking place in colleges and universities all around the country, denying them the privilege, freely afforded leftist speakers, prevented by student instigators to speak about the natural laws of God. University administrators, the media, and state houses. In Washington, the US Congress, Senate, and US Supreme Court are not sympathetic to Christian ethics and moral values, and many times did not stand with the people of faith, and in many cases, denying Christians their constitutional right to free expression and freedom of religion in a public square. The Bible has now achieved the dubious distinction of being labeled a manual for "hate speech" because it explicitly speaks out against the murder of the innocents, homosexual marriage, and transgenderism, and choices in direct disparity to biblical teaching and speaking out against these perversions will find you in the cross hairs of the district attorney and being prosecuted, as already is the case in Canada.

The loss of freedom of speech and freedom of religion became for me more problematic as my faith grew stronger. To imagine a future without Christianity, I quote John Witte of Emory University School of Law who wrote "Christianity and Democracy" in 1992,

> Christianity and democracy complement each other." Christianity provides democracy with a system of beliefs that integrates its concerns for liberty and responsibility, individuality, and community. Democracy provides Christianity with a system of government that balances its concerns for human dignity, social pluralism, and progress. This complementarity has brought Christianity and democracy together and placed Christianity in the vanguard of early modern democratic revolutions in the West and spawned a new wave of democratic revolutions breaking out around the world.

I am committed to forge ahead, defending the Christian worldview in the face of an increasingly un-Christian worldview supported by the liberal media, liberal judges, and legislators and even liberal Christian denominations, who actively encourage alternative lifestyles, and falling in line behind the postmodern theology of no absolutes. In recent years, there have been Protestant congregations and synagogues who appointed gay and lesbian rabbis and ministers to be their senior pastors and church leaders, which needs a heretical interpretation of Scripture.

The Roman Catholic Church is under great strain, intensified by the sexual abuses of children in Catholic schools and parishes and predator priests. Viable parishes are dwindling at an alarming rate and forcing some dioceses to close or merge 50 percent of their parishes. Nevertheless, even with all these issues of priests abusing children and seminarians abused by bishops and even cardinals, accused of cover-ups committed by the Catholic hierarchy, the church called by Jesus will not be overcome by Satan (Matt. 16:18).

St. Paul wrote in Ephesians 6:10–12,

> Finally, be strong in the LORD and in his mighty power. Put on the full armor of God, so that you can take your stand against the devil's schemes. For our struggle is not against flesh and blood, but against the rulers, against the authorities, against the powers of this dark world and against the spiritual forces of evil in the heavenly realms.

Realizing the power of evil and the battle waged by the powers of this dark world has reinforced my desire to battle it out even more. The question persists; is there an alternative to this madness, and where can we turn to? When the Lord Jesus said in the Gospel of John 6:53, "Unless you eat my flesh and drink my blood, you will have no life in you," and in 6:66, "From this time on, many of His Disciples turned back and no longer followed Him. Jesus asked the twelve, do you not want to leave too?"

And Peter said to the Lord, "To whom shall we go? You have the words of eternal life. We believe and know that You are the Holy One of God." Jesus is the answer, and when we abandon what Jesus taught, our lives and our nation will, like a house built on sinking sand, go into a tailspin.

"And I tell you that you are Peter, and on this rock, I will build my church, and the gates of Hades will not overcome it" (Matt. 16:18). His church will prevail, in what form or whether it be in small congregations, or in megachurches, with few believers in small churches or still worshipping in cathedrals still is to be seen. Just like Peter asked the Lord, "Where shall we go?" so I am asking myself the same question two thousand years later, and the answer needs to be same.

Would I be nourished more in a church, which serves "unconsecrated wonder bread" and unfermented Welches grapefruit juice for communion? This dilution of the Blessed Sacrament was pointed out by the Apostle Paul in 1 Corinthians 11:29–30, "For those who eat and drink without discerning the body of Christ eat and drink judgment on themselves. That is why many among you are weak and sick, and several you have fallen asleep." My firm conviction is, Christianity arose by the power of the Blessed Sacrament, and it will die by the serving of unconsecrated Wonder Bread, and only once a month as a symbol of an event that took place in Palestine two thousand years ago.

Flannery O'Connor, a Christian writer said, "If it is only a symbol, then the hell with it." A life serving inmate sang a song in one of our Alpha sessions in prison, "Jesus Christ the Lord is real; Jesus is real to me. He gave me the victory, so many people doubt Him, but I can't live without Him, that is why I love Him so, because Jesus is real to me." Jesus is real to me in the Blessed Sacrament, and I also cannot live without the nourishment of His body and His blood and is very real to me in the bread and wine. In all of history, from Abraham to Jesus, and from the beginning of the Common Era to the present time, persecution from atheistic governments has always been and continues around the world, but as the Lord Jesus told Peter, "The gates of Hades will not prevail against it."

The Apostles prayed and huddle together in the upper room after the crucifixion, but when the sound like the blowing of a violent wind came from heaven and filled the whole house, and tongues of fire came to rest on each of them, and all were filled with the Holy Spirit and began to speak in other tongues, and they went out into all the world to share the Good News. The eleven disciples went to Galilee, to the mountain where Jesus had told them to go.

> When they saw him, they worshiped him;
> but some doubted. Then Jesus came to them and
> said, "All authority in heaven and on earth has
> been given to me. Therefore make disciples of
> all nations, baptizing them in the name of the
> Father and of the Son and of the Holy Spirit, and
> teaching them to obey everything I have com-
> manded you. And surely, I am with you always,
> to the very end of the age. (Matt. 28:16–20)

Twenty years of attending a Protestant church and studying the theology, they adhere to convinced me that as the Apostle Peter said to the Lord, "Where shall I go?" The Catholic Church, with all its warts and blemishes, is still the Church that is the "Bride of Christ." In me, there was always that longing for the body and blood of Christ, and the quiet adoration and the presence of the heart of Jesus. All the fiery sermons and enthusiastic displays of worship in a Protestant church cannot satisfy my inner hunger for the Lord's real presence in the Eucharistic celebration of the body and blood of Christ and to be in communion with my Lord Jesus.

The nourishment I receive from the body and blood of Christ is the vital sustenance in my walk with my Lord and keeps me on serving Him. I am sure, just as the Apostle Paul wrote, I can do all things through Him who strengthens me in sharing the Lord with those who have fallen away. Evil continues to darken their future and robs them of the life that the Lord Jesus has prepared for them. We can hear very spiritual sermons and find friendships in other denominations, but there always be a God-sized emptiness within us that can only be filled with the body and blood of Christ when we receive the Eucharist in the Blessed Sacrament. "That is why many among you are weak and sick, and several you have fallen asleep" (1 Cor. 11:30). Falling asleep cannot be the way for the church to stay vibrant and draw more people to Jesus. Abraham Lincoln observed, if people sleeping in church would lay out end to end, they would be much more comfortable. I can personally vouch to that fact, sitting in the choir loft for thirty years, overlooking the people sitting in the pews, I noticed a lot of sleeping going on.

Rick Warren from Saddleback Church in California wrote *The Purpose Driven Life*, and on the first page, he poses the question, "What on earth am I here for?" To worship God and bring glory and honor to Him.

Ephesians 2:10 further answers that question:

We are God's workmanship, created in Christ Jesus to do good works, which God has in advance prepared for us to do, and I am convinced, that apart from the Lord, no one will enjoy life while on this Earth and everlasting joy in His presence. Catherine of Sienna wrote in the fourteenth century, "The way to heaven is heaven." If we follow the way, the truth, and the life, "Jesus saith unto him, I am the way, the truth, and the life: no man cometh unto the Father, but by me" (John 14:6). There is no other way to heaven but be nourished by the bread from heaven, and only then can we live in this world, but not be of this world. "I have given them your word and the world has hated them, for they are not of the world any more than I am of the world" (John 17:14).

There are people who diligently study the Bible. "You study the Scriptures diligently because you think that in them you have eternal life. These are the very Scriptures that testify about me, yet you refuse to come to me to have life" (John 5:39–40 NIV). Many are active in church and attend Bible studies and are very sincere in their faith, but as Revelation 2:2–5 tells us,

> I know your deeds, your hard work and your perseverance. I know that you cannot tolerate wicked people, that you have tested those who claim to be apostles but are not, and I have found them false. You have persevered and have endured hardships for my name and have not grown weary. Yet I hold this against you: You have forsaken the love you had at first.

The first love is serving the least of these, not a self-serving faith, or as Martin Luther wrote: "We are saved by grace alone, but not by grace that is alone," and only when we practice the JOY (*Jesus* first, *others* second, and *you* last), is it possible to live life to the fullest, that is the first love the Lord speaks about in Revelation 2:4.

I do not have a theological degree or an ordination from any denomination, but what I do have is a mission to share the love of my Lord Jesus with all that the Lord has given me. Studying the Word and serving my beloved Jesus for the last twenty-five years in many seminars, geriatric training, and volunteer spiritual care capacities, and I still physically and mentally am able to serve God by His grace. The first fifty years of my life, the Lord carried me every step of the way, from inception to my first steps and every step thereafter, and by His grace, many doors have opened where I was privileged to serve, and still serve.

I have met highly educated clergy who seem to have lost their first love, and therefore unable to connect with the average congregants sitting in the pews, especially the not so highly educated or not so enlightened.

But for me and my house, as Joshua told the Israelites, we serve the Lord. Joshua chapter 24 has had a significant impact on my life. Joshua tells his people to decide, whether you want to serve the old way or are you serving the Lord in the promised land the new way, leaving false gods behind. The Pharisees and the Sadducees sat in high places but did not lift a finger.

The Power of the Cross

The story is told of a rambunctious little boy who had been expelled from several private schools, with the parents at a loss of what to do, and as a last resort, enrolled the boy in a Catholic school, and his grades rapidly improved. The father, curious what caused this rapid improvement, asked the boy, and he explained, on my first day in class, "I looked up, and I saw a body nailed to the cross, and I knew, they were serious, I better behave so I will not suffer the same fate."

We all might be tempted to follow the easy road that leads to destruction. "Enter through the narrow gate. For wide is the gate and broad is the road that leads to destruction, and many enter through it. But small is the gate and narrow the road that leads to life, and only a few find it" (Matt. 7:13).

Quoting Robert Frost, "The Road Not Taken" is an ambiguous poem that allows the reader to think about choices in life, whether to go with the mainstream or take the road that leads to life. Life is a journey, and Frost's poem highlights those times in life when a decision must be made. Which way will I go? "Two roads diverged in some wood, and I—I took the one less traveled by, and that has made all the difference."

The road that I have chosen in my journey has not been easy, at times being ridiculed, being shunned, and being dead tired after visiting hospital patients, praying with the patients from diverse backgrounds and speaking in different languages, ministering to inmates in prisons and overworked staff.

I rely heavily on Philippians 4:13: "I can do all things through Him who gives me the strength."

"In God, whose word I praise, in the Lord, whose word I praise, 11 in God I trust and am not afraid. What can man do to me? And if my God is with me, who can be against me, and the Lord has strengthened me" (Ps. 56:10–11 NIV).

There have been moments when I asked God "Lord, what are you thinking" or like the Fiddler on the Roof, called out to God, "Was that necessary?" Did that have to be? But I believe with all my heart that this is exactly where the Lord wanted me to be, and without any doubt, these situations have stretched and taken me much further than if I would have just attended faithfully church on Sunday, or occasionally read Scripture. Faith comes alive when it is lived. The disciples who followed the Lord Jesus have seen faith in action, and after the Lord's departure, have taken up the Cross and followed His instructions.

Mission to Unite Christians

I am deeply committed to make people of faith aware of the danger of division, and the consequences for Christians being indifferent to the danger of slinking from a Christian worldview toward a secular worldview with a social relativism construct of no absolute truths, eventually leading to nihilism, which negates faith and reason, and moral principles. The Apostle Paul gave us clear instructions in Ephesians 4:1–6:

> As a prisoner for the LORD, then, I urge
> you to live a life worthy of the calling you have

received. Be completely humble and gentle; be patient, bearing with one another in love. Be completely humble and gentle. Make every effort to keep the unity of the Spirit through the bond of peace. There is one body and one Spirit, just as you were called to one hope when you were called; one LORD, one faith, one baptism; one God and Father of all, who is over all and through all and in all.

As the disciples were empowered by the power of the Holy Spirit, so may the Holy Spirt empower me to speak up as the apostles did on Pentecost.

When the day of Pentecost came, they were all together in the Upper Room, when suddenly a sound like the blowing of a violent wind came from heaven and filled the room. They saw tongues of fire that separated and came to rest on each of them. All of them were filled with the Holy Spirit and began to speak in other tongues as the Spirit enabled them. (Acts 2:1–4)

Then Peter stood up with the Eleven, raised his voice and addressed the crowd: "Fellow Jews and all of you who live in Jerusalem, let me explain this to you; listen carefully to what I say. These people are not drunk, as you suppose. It is only nine in the morning! No, this is what was spoken by the prophet Joel:" In the last days, God says, I will pour out my Spirit on all people. Your sons and daughters will prophesy, your young men will see visions, your old men will dream dreams. Even on my servants, both men and women, I will pour out my Spirit in those days, and they will prophesy. Peter spoke so powerfully that three thousand were added to their number that day. The Disciple proclaimed and practiced what the Lord has taught them (Acts 2:14–18)

The day I invited the Lord Jesus into my heart, my fear of praying publicly, or speaking in front of a church full of parishioners had evaporated, and I was able to share the Good News on Hemingway Boulevard in Brooklyn, New York, Connecticut prisons, and hospitals.

The Book of Acts is not called Acts for nothing, meaning, "do something." The followers of Christ did exactly that for the following three hundred years, spoke about the truth and the way, even when threatened with imminent death by the Roman rulers, but against all odds they prevailed.

Christianity underwent a fundamental shift in its ecclesiastic independence after Emperor Constantine proclaimed the Edict of Milan in 313. I would argue that that was the beginning of the secular powers gaining influence over the church of Jesus Christ, some even to this day. The Sword of Damocles hanging over the churches in the form of "tax exemptions" and the power of censorship with what can be preached from the pulpit. In truth, Christian churches are extremely comfortable with this arrangement, not to be too cynic, but it smacks of what is commonly known as "One hand washed the other" just to get along. In recent years, megachurches have adopted a feel-good theology, to draw mammoth crowds to supply the funds to build and support Romanesque arenas, and this only is possible because of freedom from taxation.

Relying heavily on Matthew 7:7–8, "Ask and it will be given to you; seek and you will find; knock and the door will be opened to you. For everyone who asks receives; the one who seeks finds; and to the one who knocks, the door will be opened." Preaching a Gospel of prosperity in large opulent venues, even sports arenas, dazzling worshippers with elaborate light shows, and professional singers, endlessly repeating of the same stanzas. Charismatic orators delivering a message according to the gospel of prosperity, video-streaming messages to giant screens to multiple storefront houses of worship across the state, or on national TV. Jesus did not promise His followers only contentment and material riches. He told His followers, "You will have trouble, I came to seek and safe the lost, and I came to serve, not to be served."

The church that the Lord spoke of to Peter has withstood against all odds and could not be eradicated by all despots who tried it. "And I tell you, you are Peter, and on this rock, I will build my church, and the gates of hell shall not prevail against it" (Matt. 16:18). The temple was torn down because God allowed it; otherwise, His chosen people would have been just so happy to sit in prominent places in the temple, or the temple gates and look spiffy in their finest Phylacteries and Tassels, just like can be seen in our present-day churches. The Pharisees would not have had any inclination to disperse into the diaspora, which proved the perfect venue for the apostles to spread the Gospel. God works in mysterious ways; the heathen Romans build the roads, the Jews dispersed on those roads into the diaspora and met in synagogues, and the apostles preached in the synagogues. We read in the New Testament how Paul went to the synagogues to preach and teach. "And after taking some food, he regained his strength. Saul spent several days with the disciples in Damascus. At once he began to preach in the synagogues that Jesus is the Son of God" (Acts 9:19–20 NIV).

It was not until Constantine elevated the church of the way to the state religion, and under the influence of his mother, St. Helena, erected large structures in the Holy Land. In the Middle Ages, European emperors exacted taxes from the peasants to build cathedrals, and the papacy relied on indulgences to shore up their finances and build St. Peter's Cathedral. Charismatic and reformed denominations are coaxing their faithful to open their wallets and drop one-hundred-dollar bills into the offering plates with the assurance that the Lord will reward them hundredfold for their generosity. Even Wall Street would not be so brazen and promise such heavenly returns on their investments. At this point, I would like to reiterate what the Lord said to the woman at the well to the question of where she should worship. The Jews telling us we must worship in

Jerusalem, and my people, meaning the Samaritans, telling us we must worship on this mountain, meaning Mount Gerizim.

> "Sir," the woman said, "I can see that you are a prophet. Our ancestors worshiped on this mountain, but you Jews claim that the place where we must worship is in Jerusalem." "Woman," Jesus replied, "believe me, a time is coming when you will worship the Father neither on this mountain nor in Jerusalem. You Samaritans worship what you do not know; we worship what we do know, for salvation is from the Jews. Yet a time is coming and has now come when the true worshipers will worship the Father in the Spirit and in truth, for they are the kind of worshipers the Father seeks. God is spirit, and his worshipers must worship in the Spirit and in truth." (John 4:19–24)

This passage in the Gospel of John has inspired me to speak up, that those within earshot hear that the body of Christ needs worshippers who will worship Him in spirit and in truth.

16

THE MALADY OF DIVISION
AND THE REFORMATION

First, I want to share the history, of the reformation and why it became the spark which supplied the fuel for the fire that engulfed all of Europe, the destruction and un-imaginable mayhem. The thirty-year war that erupted in 1618 and ended in 1648 after more than half of Europe's population was slaughtered and so weakened that it became a prime breeding ground for the plagues that beset those who had survived thirty years of warfare.

In Germany, the reformer Martin Luther's main priority was to correct the abuse of the church in Rome, which sold indulgences to shorten the time spent in purgatory, an abominable heretical practice, solely for the purpose of filling the coffers of the Vatican. Principalities, like Frederick III, elector of Saxony, found Luther's objection a convenient way to stop the practice of exacting funds from the populace to enrich the papacy, and for that reason, protected Martin Luther at Wartburg Castle. The royalties of Europe where pining for a bigger piece of the pie that Rome claimed all for itself, and Luther supplied the spark that fueled the insurgency against the power of Rome. From May 1521 to March 1522, Martin Luther was hiding out in Wartburg Castle under the assumed name of Junker Jorge (the Knight George), for his safety at the request of Frederick the Wise following Luther's excommunication by Pope Leo X and his refusal to recant at the Diet of Worms.

Frederick the Wise protected Martin Luther to further his own designs for greater influence and power. The indulgences collected and transferred to Rome, were a thorn in the flesh of Frederick the Wise for a long time and he was no longer willing to watch vast amounts of treasure leaving his domain and being transported over the Alps to Rome. The German Peasants' War (German: *Deutscher Bauernkrieg*) was a popular revolt in some German-speaking areas in Central Europe from 1524 to 1525. It failed because of intense opposition from the aristocracy, who slaughtered up to one hundred thousand of the three hundred thousand poorly armed peasants and farmers. The survivors were fined and achieved few, if any, of their goals. Like the preceding (*Bundschuh*) movement and the Hussite Wars, the war consisted of a series of both economic and religious revolts in which peasants and farmers, often supported by anabaptist clergy, took the lead.

The German Peasants' War was Europe's largest and most widespread popular uprising prior to the French Revolution of 1789. The fighting was at its height in the middle of 1525. The peasants mistakenly believed that Martin Luther would influence the nobility in their favor but were bitterly disappointed when Luther sided with the oppressors.

Soon thereafter, the Schmalkaldik Wars erupted from 1546 until 1547 between the forces of Emperor Charles V of the Holy Roman Empire, commanded by the Duke of Alba and the Duke of Saxony, and the Lutheran Schmalkaldik League within the domains of the Holy Roman Empire.

In 1618, the war of the Reformation broke out and continued for thirty years until 1648, by which time Europe was so devastated that half the European population were slaughtered or died of starvation. In 1648, the warring powers finally came to the realization that if the fighting did not cease, there would be nobody left alive to negotiate with. Hence the Treaty at Worms in 1648 was signed. Sadly, soon after the treaty was signed, the plague known as the Black Death broke out and devastated half of the remaining population. In my hometown, when my father was digging ditches for drainage pipes, he unearthed mass graves, where substantial number of bones from that period were hurriedly buried, and later, a church had been built in memory of all those who perished.

A House Divided Cannot Stand

The famous aphorism "a house divided against itself cannot stand" is found in each of the Synoptic Gospels (Matt. 12:22–32; Luke 11:14–23; Mark 3:22–29) and is true today as it was in the time Jesus walked this Earth.

I have seen in many conversations with my Evangelical friends, a deep-seated antipathy toward the Catholic church, some even resorting to asking Catholic priests and even bishops, if they are a Christian, and have they been saved. Leading evangelical TV preachers openly refer to Catholic Christians as heretics. How could such division not be harmful to Christianity? Christians in our day are already battling secular forces describing Christianity as irrelevant and not useful in a postmodern society, and out of tune for opposing gay marriages and alternative lifestyles, and recently, transgenderism. The Catholic Church has consistently refused to join the chorus of the postmodern theology "*If It feels good, then do it.*" I find myself defending the Catholic church, as I agree with the rich Catholic traditions. In most conversations, it reveals a total lack of understanding of the teaching of the Catholic Magisterium by Protestant brothers and sisters. An irritative point of friction is the narrative of the "Magnificat" in Luke 1:43,

> "And whence is this to me, that the mother of my LORD should come to me? Mary the mother of God."

> And Mary said: "My soul glorifies the LORD and my spirit rejoices in God my Savior, for he has been mindful of the humble state of his servant. From now on all generations will call me blessed, for the Mighty One has done wonderful things for me—holy is his name. (Luke 1:46–49)

"Hail Mary, full of grace. Our Lord is with you. Blessed are thou among women, and blessed is the fruit of the womb, Jesus. Holy Mary, Mother of God, pray for us sinners, now and at the hour of our death. Amen." This prayer is verbatim from the Gospel of Luke. Protestants and Catholics alike in North America celebrate Christmas, and what would Christmas be like without Mary and no baby Jesus? Christians in many other parts of the world do not wait for the Macy's invented Santa Claus sliding down the chimney to stuff the stockings hanging from the fireplace. Christians living in other nations celebrate the Lord Jesus being the gift to the world. St. Nicholas of Myra was the bishop who handed out gifts to those who were good. Those who were not good received a little swipe from a branch. This was the custom in Germany when I was a child and celebrated St. Nicholas Day on December 6.

There are few differences between Christian denominational creeds and mission statements that divide us, but more theological devotions unite us. Jesus Himself admonished the disciples:

> "Teacher," said John, "we saw someone driving out demons in your name and we told him to stop, because he was not one of us." "Do not stop him," Jesus said. "For no one who does a miracle in my name can in the next moment say anything bad about me, for whoever is not against us is for us. Truly I tell you, anyone who gives you a cup of water in my name because you belong to the Messiah will certainly not lose their reward." (Mark 9:38–41)

Example: The springbok, native to Africa, is an extremely alert and swift animal, able to outrun about any predator and often impossible even for a lion or other big cat to catch up to, but when they are fighting each other, they are oblivious to the approaching danger and easily devoured. The secular culture has been successfully relegating Christian denominations to limit their evangelization activities to their denominational gathering places and are not able to exert influence over the declining cultural moral values. The public's subjective relativism of no absolute truths makes it imperative for Christians to stand together through increasing their ecumenical ministries. The Lord has granted me opportunities as a volunteer chaplain to reach out to all denominations. The prayer attributed to St. Francis has inspired me, as it has already inspired millions of people throughout the last one thousand years.

> Where there is hatred, let me sow love; where there is injury, pardon; where there is doubt, faith; where there is despair, hope; where there is darkness, light; where there is sadness, joy; O Divine Master grant that I may not so much seek to be consoled as to console; to be understood as to understand; to be loved as to love. For it is in giving that we receive; it is in pardoning that we are pardoned; and it is in dying that we are born to eternal life.

Was the Reformation a Blessing or a Curse?

The Reformation has been costly, especially for the peasant population beyond what Luther, Thomas Münzer, Heidrich Zwingli, or Calvin could have imagined, or wanted, but religious divisions have in all of history contributed to mass killings on all continents.

On the positive side, the Reformation encouraged the general population to become more literate and educated in Scripture, mostly because of Johannes Guttenberg's invention of the printing press, which made it possible for people to have Bibles available in their own language. But what is conveniently omitted is the illiteracy rate at the time of Gutenberg's invention and that only a small number of the population was literate enough to read printed material. Martin Luther translated the Latin Vulgate into German by combining twenty-two different dialects into what is referred to as the German high language. The written words before 1550 were exclusively written in Latin, and only a few outside of monastery walls were able read Latin. Documents up to the late 1500 were only written in Latin, and there is even suspicion that many regents were illiterate and could not read the documents set before them for their signature. From the late 1600 century on, the literacy rate improved rapidly throughout Europe. The Catholic church continued to publish Scriptures in the Vulgate (Latin). Latin Masses continued until the mid-nineteen sixties, when the Second Vatican Council allowed the Mass to celebrated in the vernacular of the people.

The Reformation, for all its touted positives, proved to be a negative for Christianity. The weakened and exhausted Christian European nations, their finances depleted by sixty years of warfare against each other were unable to halt the Islamic expansion into the Balkans, which became a serious threat to the Holy Roman Empire, led at that time by the Habsburg monarchy and the Polish-Lithuanian Commonwealth. The Ottoman Turks only ceased to be a menace after the European Christian world united, and the Ottomans lost the battle of Vienna against the joint efforts of the Habsburg and Polish Army and the Holy Roman Emperor Leopold I. On a more personal level, the division between the Catholic and Protestant church also wreaked havoc in family relations well into the 1960s and 1970s, when Catholic families still warned their children to avoid playing with Protestant children and vice versa.

Marriages were a particularly thorny issue as the populations shifted because of the displacements during and after WWII in Europe. In America, more of the diverse population intermarried because of the accelerated immigration from Europe's war-torn nations. The Catholic insistence that annulments can only be granted by a tribunal, chaired by a Bishop, supplied a steady flow of funds to the diocesan treasury. Annulments also required a Protestant partner to convert to Catholicism, which many Protestants refused to do, effectively creating the second largest denomination in the US, made up of former Catholics who found the annulment process too cumbersome and a considerable financial burden for the already stretched budget of a blended family. The remarriages of the wealthy, especially when Edward Kennedy divorced and remarried within a brief time, left the impression that the rich receive preferential treatment form the church hierarchy.

The reunification of the splintered Christian Faith Community is desperately needed to survive the onslaught of the secular world, and the increasing Islamization of Europe. Many Protestants are convinced that Catholics are not saved and worship Mary more than Jesus, depicting them as heretics and certainly not eligible to enter heaven. John Fullerton MacArthur Jr. is an American pastor and author, known for his internationally syndicated Christian teaching radio program *Grace to You*, and Richard Albert Mohler Jr., an American historical theologian, president of the Southern Baptist Theological Seminary in Louisville, Kentucky. Both known as "America's most influential evangelicals," they are prime examples of the divided Christianity in America. Both Bible scholars refused to meet with Pope John Paul as he requested on his visit to the US. Their explanation was that they considered the pope the anti-Christ and a heretic.

I conducted a Christian worship service a few years back when a woman jumped out of her seat and screamed, "I am leaving, because I am a Catholic, and not a Christian." What I am trying to point out here is that this kind of division will continue to harm Christianity and make all Christians more vulnerable to the humanistic forces, solidly united into marginalizing Christian influence. The steady decline of morality and ethics among the population is living proof of the success by the "secular worldview crowd." St. Theresa of Calcutta wrote: "We cannot save the entire world, but we can save one by one." I am not insinuating that everyone will be saved as many Evangelicals understand the word "being saved," but we can be the light that shines before the entire world.

"Let your light so shine before men, that they may see your good works, and glorify your Father which is in heaven" (Matt. 5:16). Atheists may be very honorable people and many live by the golden rule, which is a rule of ethical conduct referring to Matthew 7:12 and Luke 6:31: "Do to others as you would have them do to you." Something similar appears in every major religion and ethical philosophy; in Hindu, Jewish, Buddhist, Confucian, and Zoroastrian versions, it appeared already 3,500 years earlier. There were rulers in all of history who interpret this rule differently; "He who has the gold rules." In the US, public schools have taught Evolutionary Theory already for ninety years, are and still teaching that we are children not created by God, and therefore we no longer need to believe in a Creator God. This begs the question then, "Why are the Ten Commandments still the basis for our legal system?" The Ten Commandments have not changed since Moses brought them down from Mt. Sinai, and they will not change, unless the forces opposed to God become a more powerful entity, and thus, able to remove any vestiges of Christianity. The laws of all Christian western societies rest on the foundational decrees of the Ten Commandments.

What would Christianity look like today, if all Christian churches would worship the Lord in one accord and share the bread and wine together? Well, we may find the answer in Matthew 26:26–30:

> While they were eating, Jesus took bread, and when he had given thanks, he broke it and gave it to his disciples, saying, "Take and eat; this is my body." Then he took the cup, and when he had given thanks, he gave it to them, saying, "Drink from it, all of you. This is my blood of the covenant, which is poured out for many for the forgiveness of sins. I tell you, I will not drink from this fruit of the vine from now on until that day when I drink it new with you in my Father's kingdom." When they had sung a hymn, they went out to the Mount of Olives.

Question: If Protestant denominations believe in the miracle of the resurrection, then, why not in the miracle of the transubstantiation? Protestant churches claim, "Sola Scriptura," but are splintered worldwide into forty thousand different denominations, and observe different traditions, but accuse the Catholic church of elevating traditions above Scripture. Would Jesus really encourage His followers to build a new hierarchy that would resemble the "*Whitewashed Tombs*" that he accused the Sadducees and Pharisees of making up rules but not lifting a finger to help those who do all the heavy lifting.

Erecting gigantic cathedrals requiring enormous amounts of money to build and support, which are now scarcely attended. I have a difficulty finding anywhere in the Gospels the verses and the instructions to preach the Gospel of prosperity in ten-thousand-dollar suits and one-thousand-dollar sneakers prominently displayed by megachurch preachers. A more recent trend is on the opposite side of the spectrum, preaching in blue jeans and T-shirts, resembling rock stars in their mod outfits, trying to be more appealing to a younger crowd. The entertainment element in many Sunday morning Church services resemble rock concerts more than a worship service. Earsplitting sound levels and psychedelic light shows swooning over giant screens mounted on walls surrounding the worshippers.

By contrast, I personally must find a place where I can worship my God in quiet adoration and contemplation, one which allows me to hear myself think and focus all my attention on my God. As to that end, I rediscovered the Catholic church where I can sit still and hear Him speak to me, knowing that the Lord's first language is silence: *"Is that still small voice."* That we only hear in the stillness of contemplation. How can the trend of Catholics and Protestants leaving pews empty, and the shuttering of church doors be reversed? Large numbers of Catholics have left the Catholic church because of the annulment process necessary before remarrying after their divorce to be in good standing to receive Holy Communion again. The annulment process gets even more complicated if a Catholic is married to a Protestant who refuses to convert to Catholicism, which then disallows the Catholic from receiving the sacrament of the Holy Communion. It Is estimated that this demand of adherence to the Catholic Magisterium is responsible for creating the second largest denomination in the US, made up of lapsed Catholics worshipping with their spouses in Protestant houses of worship. But for me, even serving in Protestant ministries, I never lost the desire and longing to receive the Blessed Sacrament, whereby my Lord abides in me and I in Him and find the nourishment I long for. "As the deer panted for the water, So my soul longest after thee" (Ps. 42:1). The years I attended only Protestant services, receiving unconsecrated wonder bread and grape juice, only remembering the Last Supper as a symbol, could not satisfy my hunger or fill the void I felt in my heart.

SECTION 4

New Direction, New Challenge

17

ANGELS SENT BY GOD

There are people who do not believe in angels, but I have been the beneficiary of so many real-life angels, being there for me, coming out of nowhere, and too numerous to chalk up to mere coincidences. Reason enough for me to believe in angels is that Scripture tells us angels sent by God, who talk to us, walk with us, and guide us. "Do not neglect to show hospitality to strangers, for thereby some have entertained angels unawares" (Heb. 13:2). Angels showed up in unique ways and unusual places, all of them unexpected. All must have been angels sent by God, or how else could I explain their sudden appearance, at the right place, the right time, when we needed them at a particular moment in our journey.

The German couple who immigrated from Vancouver, Canada, to New York who befriended us and encouraged us to attend Mass on Sundays.

A German man, who moved into an apartment across the street, his wife who gave birth to twins in Germany and followed her husband to New York, and we became close friends. This couple was deeply steeped and practicing their Catholic faith and attending weekly Mass. Hanging out together, our conversations most often centering on faith, which we intensely discussed.

The owners of companies that I worked for, who treated me with kindness and generously supported me and my family, by giving me extra food to take home and extra hours to augment the weekly paycheck.

The man who owned a meat-processing company, asking me to buy his company, even willing to finance the purchase. The corporation lawyer who provided me with top-notch counseling in the purchase agreement. All the craftsmen, too many to mention here, who did electrical work, plumbing repairs, and stainless-steel refinishing most of the processing areas to satisfy the USDA regulations. The natural organic farm who sought a processor for his natural raised animals to process their meat into natural no-nitrite meat products, which then led to a whole slew of more organic farms bringing their meat for processing. When people ask me, "Why are you so involved in ministry?" my simple answer is, "I have good reasons." The Lord has been at my side every step of the way and has blessed me in so many ways that I feel I must bless those in need of a helping hand, and according to the prayer of St. Francis, "to comfort and console, not to be consoled, but console those who need to be comforted."

To name just a few more, the pastor of the congregational church who encouraged us to take part in the New York City Homeless Mission. The man who approached me to come to the youth prison with him. The Masonic Hospital chaplain who placed the ad for spiritual care volunteers. The pastor in Puerto Rico who invited Roswitha and me to preach in his church. The hospital chaplain at Middlesex Hospital who assigned us to pastoral care. The lady who approached Roswitha and me in Kennebunk Port, engaging us for two hours in a spiritual conversation about our faith.

18

RETIRING

Blessings That Came My Way

After being employed full time for fifty-three years, and for most of those years, working six days a week as it is customary in the meat business, achieving everything I ever hoped or dreamed of, I honestly could not attribute any of it to my own wisdom and strength, but only by God's grace. Married to my wife Roswitha for fifty-eight years and blessed with three healthy children, five grandchildren, and now five great-grandchildren.

On the economic side, the vocational trade education that was available to me and the gathering of more knowledge through working in different German regions. The urge to emigrate to America, and the need for experienced sausage makers in New York City's meat processing companies, offering me immediate work even without any English language skills. The coincidence that many meat-processing plants happened to be owned and operated by either Germans, or German-speaking Jewish people, many themselves emigrants. The call of a former employer in need of an experienced manager for his business and a lucrative offer to join him. It proved to be more than just earning a good salary, but also, it supplied me the training and business savvy I was still lacking and could not have gained anywhere else. The opportunity to buy a sausage manufacturing business, realizing a dream of mine to manufacture sausage products on a retail and wholesale level. Purchasing the company without using any of my own financial resources and financed with a no-interest loan, which I was able to pay back within five years. The business prospered, providing me with twenty-seven years of uninterrupted flow of income.

At the age of sixty-five, I was contemplating and seeking a way to retire, when at the same time, my wife Roswitha was diagnosed with breast cancer, requiring more care as she was battling her cancer. This made the sale of the company more urgent, and by the grace of God, the company was sold on February 11, 2011. I am often reminded of the passage in John 14:16–18, "And I will ask the Father, and he will give you another advocate to help you and be with you forever—I will not leave you orphans, the Holy Spirit will lead you and guide you in all truth and righteousness."

There are so many more miracles and instances that I will share some other time.

19

NEW DIRECTION, NEW CHALLENGE

In the fall of 2018, my wife and I felt a need to take a break from all our activities and get away for a mini vacation. We remembered the place in Southern Maine where we stayed two years earlier on a mini vacation. Spontaneously, we called the Franciscan House in Kennebunk Port, a hotel with extensive grounds and scenery and a quiet atmosphere for reflection and relaxation. On short notice, a room was miraculously available, and the next morning, we were on our way to Kennebunk Port, Maine.

The hotel, an extension of a Lithuanian Franciscan Monastery, which we already had stayed in two years earlier, and we found again the peace and quiet we were seeking. This trip turned out a little different from our earlier stay. We took a walk on the trails leading to Kennebunk Cove, dotted with many stations of the cross and replicas of the grottos of the Lady of Fatima and the Lady of Lourdes along the paths. Walking for about two hours, exhausted and in need to give our poor old legs a rest, we found a bench in the shade of a big tree to sit down on, soaking in the warm morning sun, when suddenly a car stopped in front of us, and a lady opened the car window, and very enthusiastically wished us a good morning. She then drove a little further on, stopped, and put the car in reverse and came to a halt right in front of us.

Getting out of the car, she engaged us in a very long, intense theological discussion about the Catholic divorce annulment process, necessary to receive the Blessed Sacrament. It turned out, the lady was a local artist and a writer of spiritual books and was desperate to tell someone that she was depressed because of her impending eightieth birthday. She thanked us for our patience and handed us two of her hand-painted bookmarks with a Bible verse in the front and her email address in the back. We said our goodbyes, without any indication that we would ever meet again, and yet, the following morning, as we were enjoying our breakfast with another couple we had met two years earlier at the same hotel, the lady we met the day before approached our table and asked if she could join us.

All five of us were then engaged in a lively theological discussion about the Catholic Magisterium and Canon Law pertaining to annulments of failed marriages. She casually mentioned that she had written three books that where available through Amazon, and that same evening, I logged on to Amazon and ordered her books, and to our surprise, the books had been delivered to our house in Connecticut before we arrived back home two days later with a nice note attached, expressing her delight in finding someone open enough to engage in a theological discussion about the Catholic Magisterium. Truth being, I also was eager to engage in a spiritual discussion on faith.

The lady that stopped her car in front of us must have been an angel sent our way by God, considering being four hours away from our home, making reservations on a whim, and then, after a long walk, stopping to rest our legs. Meeting this strange lady provided me with the stimulus to seriously consider writing about my spiritual life. It never ceases to amaze me how the Lord works in mysterious ways, sending unexpected strangers my way. In the Book of Numbers, God did send an angel to reroute Balaam's path on the road to Moab. Balaam could not see the angel, but his donkey did and spoke to Balaam (Num. 22:23).

I have been aware of how the Holy Spirit worked in my life, but after giving my life to the Lord Jesus, a strong desire came over me to increase my knowledge of the Gospel and to share the Good News in all the places the Lord will lead me and to share God's love and the hope we have in Christ Jesus. Whether in prisons, hospitals, mental institutions, or the homeless, I know that the Lord has blessed me beyond my wildest imagination. I see people in a whole different light, seeing the face of Jesus in them, and as the Lord said in Matthew 25:40, "The King will reply, 'Truly I tell you, whatever you did for one of the least of these brothers and sisters of mine, you did for me." Every moment I am sharing the Good News far exceeds anything that I could have gained by watching TV or the internet. "Now to him who can do immeasurably more than all we ask or imagine, according to his power that is at work within us, to him be glory in the church and in Christ Jesus throughout all generations" (Eph. 3:20–21 NIV). The Lord has given me a life filled with a purpose that is more than I could never have imagined.

SECTION 5

Postmodern Theology

20

CHANGING CHRISTIAN WORLDVIEW

Today we are witnessing the negative impact that a moral-relativistic worldview has on American culture. Colleges and universities engage in indoctrinating and brainwashing generations into thinking that absolute truths are irrelevant in a relativistic modern society. The generation born after the year 2000 lack a clear understanding of their role in life, their identity, even questioning their God-given gender, whether they are male or female. The phenomenon of transgenderism has resulted in states legalizing the right for adult males to relieve themselves next to females in a *girl's bathroom* by claiming to be a transgender female. This has led to the gender identity crisis, "Who am I?" Am I a male or a female, leading to psychiatric or surgical interventions? *Primal Screams*, written by Mary Eberstadt, one of the most acute and creative social observers of our times shines a much-needed light on a disturbing trend in American society. Discriminating against the traditional worldview, she illustrates how far "transgenderism," sexual created identity politics has progressed, human beings search for their identity. This has led to treatments of mind and body transforming pharmaceuticals, which in too many cases lead to a dependency of opioids and the root cause fueling the opioid addiction crisis.

In recent years, special attention has focused on the role doctors played in the current opioid overdose crisis in the US, with doctors overprescribing medications, claiming more lives each year than any other known disease. Not all addictions lead to death, but interfere with the normal decision-making process, and cause a lot of suffering, because of making poor choices and bad decisions. Many years ago, there were billboards on the side of the roads, prompting the public to make education a number one priority: "*A mind is too precious to waste.*" But when compromised by overprescribed medications or increased alcohol or cannabis consumption, it places the user at an extreme disadvantage in the workplace and in family relationships. The experiences I gathered in my years as an employer showed just how easy it was to recognize a worker under the influence of alcohol or drugs. Lack of punctuality and short-term memory were one of the first sign of addiction.

Medically intervening and altering a child's gender while they are still in the development stage is child abuse. Transgender people often receive medical care under the diagnosis of "gender dysphoria" and are in some cases treated with irreversible surgical intervention that exaggerates the condition. Transgenderism has encouraged parents to let their children as young as five decide their identity, not their God ordained identity, and some court cases, have already prohibited parents from interfering in their children's wish to change their gender identity from being a boy or a girl at the tender age of six years.

> So God created humankind in his own image, in the image of God he created them; male and female he created them. God saw all that he had made, and it was very good. (Gen. 1:27, 31)

> That is why a man leaves his father and mother and is united to his wife, and they become one flesh. (Gen. 2:24)

> Therefore what God has joined together, let no one separate. (Mark 10:9 NIV)

The covenant of marriage is a promise before God and the world that from this day forward, for better for worse, for richer or for poorer, in sickness and in health, to love and to cherish, till death us do part.

Overturning the God-ordained natural created order has morphed into various deviations. Many young adults are foregoing starting a family well into their thirties or opting instead for alternative lifestyle arrangements, which precludes them from procreating children. Gay and lesbian marriages have been elevated and are on equal legal footing with heterosexual marriages, and clergy are getting increasingly more nervous. When they be forced by law to perform gay and lesbian wedding ceremonies, equal to different-sex couples, without religious conscientious exemptions. Cohabitations are increasingly displacing traditional marriages. Obviously, these new arrangements are not compatible with the Christian worldview and is fuel for an even more divisive atmosphere in the political arena as well as in families when a member has chosen the popular new way of cohabiting.

I credit my success in life to not being raised in sheltered circumstances and never using mind-altering drugs to overcome stressful situations, and it was this that has never prevented me from reaching the goals I had set for my life. Goal number one was to start a family; two, to work to the best of my ability toward eventually owning my own business. Being born poor, growing up poor, marrying a poor girl, and immigrating to the US poor, with confidence and faith, I knew what I had set out to do.

My mother and father were my role models; my father's hard work and my mother's faith in her Jesus, as she always referred to Jesus and praying the Rosary enabled my mother, together with my father to raise ten children, and to overcome WWII and the dreadful aftermath. My mother's unshakable faith in her Lord Jesus was the cornerstone she leaned through the worst of her times and influenced me all my life. The secular culture, now so focused on abolishing biblical truths and natural laws, has led to a decline in ethics and moral values that no one could have fathomed sixty years ago. I am still wondering, how low can it go? There was a popular dance during the seventies, it was called the limbo, and its aim was to dance under a bar without falling backward or dislodging the bar. The bar of what is culturally acceptable has dropped below the point of no return, and further away from the biblical truth and way. Jesus said, "I am the way, the truth and the life, and any other way will not bring you to the Father."

Postmodernism rationalizes that there are no absolute absolutes and has resulted in social instability of unimaginable proportions in our society. Sexual freedoms with no restraints in sexual orientation in whatsoever combination desired has changed the social order that safeguarded the natural environment where millions of children do not grow up with a father and a mother, which has been the bedrock of societies in the East and the West and primitive societies.

The proliferation of unrestrained sexual activity has given birth to a giant federal bureaucracy, what is known as the "welfare system" that guarantees every child free food, housing, medical care, and education without any responsibility of their parents who produced the child. The increase in carjackings where mothers with babies have been pushed out of their cars by juveniles is especially worrisome, as the commandment, "Thou shalt not steal had been given by God," so that His children can go about their daily activities without fear. If the Ten Commandments and the Gospel of Jesus Christ are now substituted by the gospel of TV or the newest fad emanating out of Hollywood, then the undergirding of the family will crumble, and when that happens, the family disintegrates, society crumbles and there is already ample statistical proof for this calamity. Hillary Clinton's famous statement, "It takes a village to raise a child" is a subjective to the misguided notion of what is in a child's "best interest," and a radical departure from the traditional role that parents and only parents share responsibility in the raising of their children. It takes a village can be understood, that it takes a community of different people can authoritatively interact with everyone's children to assure that children will grow up in a safe environment. This can also be interpreted, to mean, that the entire village be involved in the raising of your children. To speak up against the new world order has moved to the forefront of the purpose for my life since I am the grandfather of five and the great-grandfather of six children.

My deepest wish for my children and grandchildren is that they will acknowledge that God is the creator of heaven and Earth, and a God of absolutes and precepts that will not change to accommodate the postmodern Christian worldview. The Lord warned His people that one cannot serve two masters, and all nations who have exchanged absolute truths for no absolute truths, have suffered catastrophic outcomes. In our private lives, the consequences of ignoring natural laws and exposing ourselves to the mantra of relativism, recalling St. Augustin who wrote, "Wrong is wrong even if everyone is doing it, and right is right even if no one is doing right."

Why Serve?

Ephesians 2:10 tells us that we are God's workmanship, created in Christ Jesus to do good works, which He had prepared in advance for us to do.

Protestant theology rests to a significant extent on Ephesians 2:4 and Galatians 2:16 that we are saved by grace alone, not by works, but Scripture also tells us that we should lay up for ourselves treasures in heaven, where neither moth nor rust doth corrupt, and where thieves do not break through nor steal (Matt. 6:20 KJV). I have yet to find in the four gospels where it is written that we are saved by grace "*alone*." "You see, that a person is justified by what he does, and not by grace alone" (James 2:24). This correlates with what Martin Luther the Reformer wrote, "We are saved by grace alone, but not by grace that is alone."

"For we must all appear before the judgment seat of Christ, so that each of us may receive what is due us for the things done while in the body, whether good or bad" (2 Cor. 5:10).

If Christ Jesus died on the Cross for me, a sinner, then why should I not feel compelled to be the hand and feet for my Lord here on earth as Theresa of Avila wrote. I have no doubts about my Lord Jesus's unconditional love, but I feel obliged to do what I can do for my brothers and sisters in need. There are times when I feel exhausted, especially when it is getting near to the end of the hospital visits, when it gets harder and more difficult even to find the right words. The fact that I have compassion and empathy to such a diverse group of people is proof that it is only possible by the grace of our Lord Jesus, and I never been fearful or afraid. The Lord reassured those He sent out in the Old and New Testament, "Fear not, for I am with you," and it is reassuring enough for me to serve the Lord wherever He leads me. For if God is with me, who can be against me? Now, at seventy-eight years of age, I do wonder sometime how long the Lord will allow me to proclaim His Word and share His love.

The Lord allowed me to work in the meat business, processing food for fifty-three years, which nourished people. St. Theresa of Calcutta said, "It is not how much you do, it is, how much you love what you do." It is virtually impossible to do your best if you do not love what you do. There are many who possess power but have not love, masquerading as a loving savior, but have no power at all to change the situation.

> Remember what happened long ago, for I am God, and there is no other; I am God, and there is none like Me. (Isa. 45:5)

> And God send His one and only Son, that anyone who believes in Him might be saved. (John 3:16 NIRV)

When the Pharisees asked the Lord Jesus about His mission on earth, He was handed the scrolls and He opened (Isa. 61) where it says His reason for coming to earth.

> The Spirit of the Sovereign Lord is on me, because the Lord has anointed me to proclaim good news to the poor. He has sent me to bind up the brokenhearted, to proclaim freedom for the captives and release from darkness for the prisoners, 2 to proclaim the year of the Lord's

favor and the day of vengeance of our God, to comfort all who mourn, 3 and provide for those who grieve in Zion—to bestow on them a crown of beauty instead of ashes, the oil of joy instead of mourning, and a garment of praise instead of a spirit of despair. (Isa. 61:1)

His mission has not changed; only now, the need is so much greater as there are now seven billion people on this earth, reassuring to me that I will never in my lifetime be running out of work for the Lord.

21

THE GREAT COMMISSION

Then the eleven disciples went to Galilee, to the mountain where Jesus had told them to go. When they saw him, they worshiped him; but some doubted. Then Jesus came to them and said, "All authority in heaven and on earth has been given to me. Therefore go and make disciples of all nations, baptizing them in the name of the Father and of the Son and of the Holy Spirit, and teaching them to obey everything I have commanded you." They could have also decided to travel the easy road and not journey down the hard road, and true to the words of Jesus, many have died on that road to heaven. (Matt. 28:17–20)

You have to lose your life to gain eternal life.

He is no fool who gives away what he cannot keep, to gain, what he cannot lose. (Jim Elliot)

And do not fear those who kill the body but are unable to kill the soul; but rather fear Him

who is able to destroy both soul and body in hell.
(Matt. 10:28)

> For if you want to save your own life, you
> will lose it; but if you lose your life for my sake,
> you will find it. (Matt. 16:25)

With these Scripture in mind, I am confident that the road I have taken in my journey of faith, considering from where I came from and how the Lord has carried me, reminds me of Martin Luther the Reformer, when he stood in front of the Imperial Diet in Worms (April 18, 1521) and spoke these words: "I neither nor will retract anything; for it cannot be either safe or honest for a Christian to speak against his conscience. Here I stand, I can do no other! God help me! Amen."

22

WHO WILL BE SAFE?

Passive Christianity can be defined as those taking part in church services on Sunday morning and weekly Bible studies, praying and expressing their concerns, only in church gatherings, but not in public forums for fear of being labeled purveyors of "hate speech" or "homophobic fundamentalists," obstructing progressive cultural changes of the secular worldview. This colossal onslaught on Christianity will require enormous public demonstrations by Christians on the scale of what Mahatma Gandhi started in India to free his people from British colonial rule. Mohandas Karamchand Gandhi was an Indian lawyer, anticolonial nationalist, and political ethicist, who led nonviolent resistance in the successful campaign to gain India's independence from British rule, the most powerful empire on Earth at the time. He was a diminutive human being, but unerringly in pursuit of his people's freedom from oppression and exploitation.

23

RISE UP, O WOMEN AND MEN OF GOD

Give heart, soul, mind, and strength. To serve the King of Kings. Rise O men of God. His Kingdom tarries long. Bring in the day of brotherhood. And end the night of wrong. Rise O men of God. The Church for you doth wait. Send forth to serve the needs of men. In Christ, our strength is great. Lift high the Cross of Christ. Tread where His feet have trod. As brothers of the Son of Man. Rise up O men of God. (William Merrill, 1914)

Men have traditionally been the spiritual leaders of the family for centuries, and together with a wife at his side, they nurtured their children. Prayer before dinner, reading Scriptures, and attending church services came to a halt when World War II broke out, and millions of men were shipped overseas far from home. This caused the women to work in factories, producing the weapons of war for the men fighting overseas. The poster of "Rosy the Riveter" with the strong arm of a woman, her kitchen towel wrapped around her head, signifying that woman are fully capable of multitasking and capable to carry out tasks that in previous years was the exclusive domain of men. Following WWII, women joined the workforce in ever-increasing numbers, adding to the family's income to buy homes under the GI loans.

Millions of returning service men entered college and universities, made possible through the Servicemen's Readjustment Act of 1944, commonly known as the GI Bill, a law that supplied a range of benefits for returning World War II veterans (commonly referred to as GIs) and where expired in 1956. Designed to reward men and women who served in military. As consumer goods became widely available, it was a time to enjoy life again. Leisure activities, whether playing golf, tennis, or TV sport broadcasts, moved to the forefront, and less time was devoted to spiritual exercises. Fathers abrogated their responsibility, passing it on to the mothers.

A good illustration is a painting by Norman Rockwell, where it shows a mother and the children dressed up and about to leave for church, and the boy gazing toward the father, sitting in his easy chair, reading the Sunday paper. The boy is getting the message that church cannot be that important because if it were his father would be leading them all to church. The boy is thinking, "This is what will do when I grow up and am a father." Rockwell's painting points out the abrogating of men's responsibilities to function as the spiritual directors of the family. Quoting Dr. Robert Royal,

> The best I can do to understand them is to think back over my own experiences. Often, I have been among the trivial and the bored. Why should I go to church when I could just as easily be bored, elsewhere? The answer might be something like, "I needed it, like I needed to take a shower."

I think many half-believing modernists do it to feel better about themselves. They may avoid confession, imagining it as a cold shower, but are still seeking a deodorant of some kind. This article from Dr. Robert Royal is a correct description of why some men are still sitting in pews on Sunday morning, but as I wrote in my book titled *A Nation Once Under God*, the absence of many fathers will create a vacuum in society that was previously occupied by a Christian worldview.

24

THE REMNANTS OF ISRAEL

T he Israelites were enslaved for four hundred years by Egypt. Nebuchadnezzar burned down the temple in 586 BC and kept the Israelites for seventy years in captivity.

> The remnant shall return, even the remnant of Jacob, unto the mighty God. (Isa. 10:21)

> I ask then: Did God reject his people? By no means! I am an Israelite myself, a descendant of Abraham, from the tribe of Benjamin. God did not reject his people, whom he foreknew. Don't you know what Scripture says in the passage about Elijah—how he appealed to God against Israel: "Lord, they have killed your prophets and torn down your altars; I am the only one left, and they are trying to kill me" And what was God's answer to him? "I have reserved for myself seven thousand who have not bowed the knee to Baal." So too, at the present time there is a remnant chosen by grace. (Rom. 11:1–5)

The Israelites called out to their God, and He did not forget them. Christians can get their cue from 2 Chronicles 7:14, "If my people, who are called by my name, will humble themselves and pray and seek my face and turn from their wicked ways, then I will hear from heaven, and I will forgive their sin and will heal their land." Faith will supply the strength and the God of Israel will secure our future.

Question is, will Christians still seek the Lord while He may be found?

"'You will seek me and find me when you seek me with all your heart. I will be found by you,' declares the LORD, 'and will bring you back from captivity'" (Jer. 29:13–14).

People must again fall in love with the Lord Jesus. "God so loved the world, that whomsoever believed in Him, shall not perish, but have eternal life."

If you want to fall deeper in love with love, I highly recommend reading the lovely stories from Catherine Doherty, who was in love with Jesus Christ. Throughout her life, Catherine chased after Christ her Bridegroom. She saw him and identified with Him. She worshipped Him and often received his real presence in the Eucharist, and she became one with Christ through an intense, painful, and loving union with his mystical Body, his Spouse, the Church.

Catherine opens her memoir saying, "You know I am in love with God, and this is a fact." Her closing words touch on the same theme: "Two people in love! When you are in love with God you will understand that he loved you first. You will enter a deep and mysterious silence, and in that silence, you will become one with the Absolute. Your oneness with God will overflow to all your brothers and sisters." The core of Doherty's spirituality was summarized in a "distillation" of the Gospel, which she called "The Little Mandate"— words that she believed she received from Jesus Christ and guided her life.

> Arise—go! Sell all you possess. Give it directly, personally to the poor. Take up My cross (their cross) and follow Me, going to the poor, being poor, being one with them, one with Me. Little—be always little! Be simple, poor, child-

like. Preach the Gospel with your life—without compromise! Listen to the Spirit. He will lead you. Do little things exceedingly well for love of Me. Love…love…love, never counting the cost. Go into the marketplace and stay with Me. Pray, fast. Pray always, fast. Be hidden. Be a light to your neighbor's feet. Go without fear into the depth of men's hearts. I shall be with you. Pray always, I will be your rest. Our hearts will find rest only when our hearts rest in God.

The day I turned my life over to Jesus, a bright light illuminated my surrounding, and I could see what the Lord wanted me to see, and He opened my heart, my mind, my soul to His way, and I finally understood John 10:8: "I am the way, the truth, and the life (light)." The Lord has shone His light unto my paths, sometimes a little dimmer, sometimes a little brighter, but without fail, bright enough for me to be able to follow in the path He had planned for me.

25

SYNOPSIS AND SUMMARY

I hope that this synopsis of my life will encourage all who have been born into humble circumstances and be a reminder that nothing is too hard for the Lord to carry out in His children what He has prepared in advance for them to do. Even when we behave like sheep who have wandered away, we need a shepherd. He will lead us to greener pastures and quiet waters.

> Praise be to the God and Father of our Lord Jesus Christ, who has blessed us in the heavenly realms with every spiritual blessing in Christ. For he chose us in him before the creation of the world to be holy and blameless in his sight. In love, He predestined us for adoption to sonship through Jesus Christ, per his pleasure and will to the praise of his glorious grace, which he has freely given us in the One he loves. (Eph. 1:3–6)

WHEN YOU THINK
THERE IS NO HOPE,
GOD SAYS
"TAKE MY HAND
AND LET ME LEAD
THE WAY.
WE CAN DO THIS
TOGETHER"

AMEN

WeAreHumanAngelsTheBook

ABOUT THE AUTHOR

Josef Herz has been president of a food processing company for twenty-seven years and volunteering in prisons and hospital ministry for twenty-four years. He was educated and trained in Germany before immigrating to the United States. Josef and his wife, Roswitha, live in Berlin, Connecticut, and have three grown children and five grandchildren.